budgetbooks

STANDARDS

7777 W. BLUEMOUND RD. P.O. BOX 13819 MILWAUKEE, WI 53213

Visit Hal Leonard Online at
www.halleonard.com

CONTENTS

AIN'T MISBEHAVIN'
from AIN'T MISBEHAVIN'

Words by ANDY RAZAF
Music by THOMAS "FATS" WALLER
and HARRY BROOKS

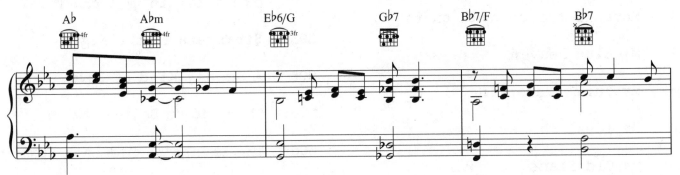

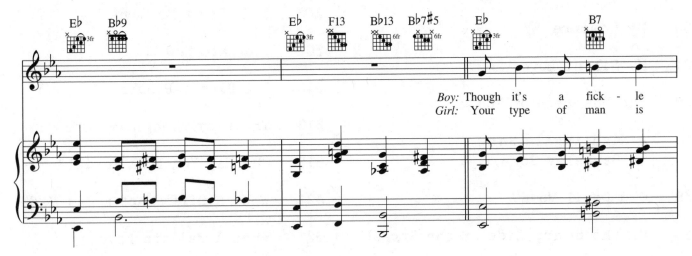

Boy: Though it's a fick - le
Girl: Your type of man is

age
rare,

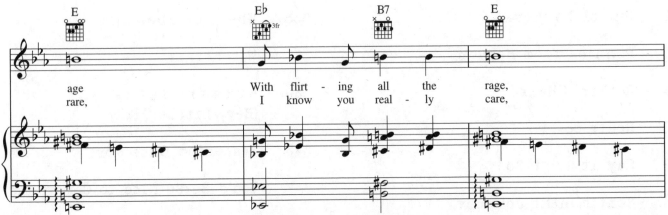

With flirt - ing all the rage,
I know you real - ly care,

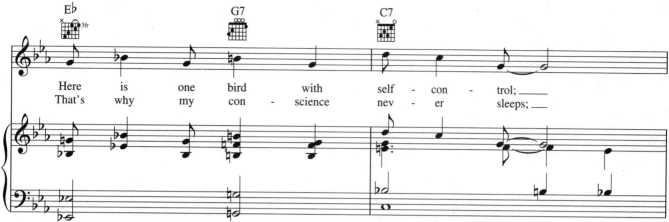

Here is one bird with self - con - trol; _____
That's why my con - science nev - er sleeps; ___

Hap - py in - side my cage.
When you're a - way some - where.

I know who I love
Sure was a luck - y

best,
day,

Thumbs down for all the rest,
When down fate sent you my way,

My love was giv - en, heart and soul; ___
And made you mine a - lone for keeps, ___

So it can stand the
Dit - to to all you

I'm through with flirt - in', it's just you I'm think - in' of. Ain't mis - be - hav - in',

I'm sav - in' my love for you. ____

Like Jack Hor - ner in the cor - ner, don't go no - where,

what do I care, Your kiss - es are worth wait - in'

THE BEST THINGS IN LIFE ARE FREE

from GOOD NEWS!

Music and Lyrics by B.G. DeSYLVA,
LEW BROWN and RAY HENDERSON

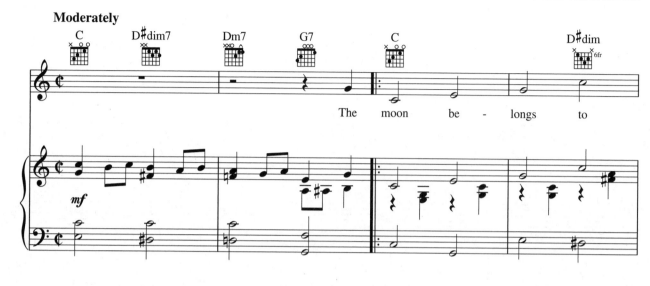

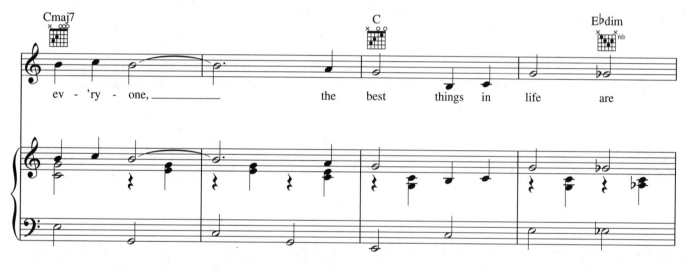

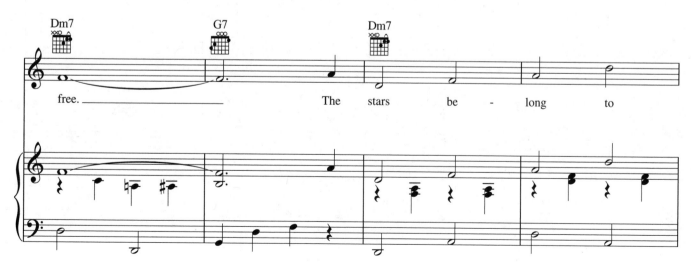

yours, they're mine! And love can come to ev - 'ry - one, the

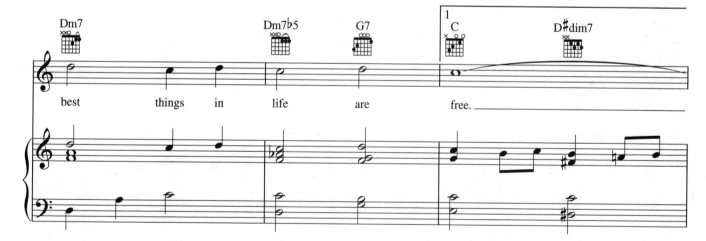

best things in life are free.

The free.

ALL BY MYSELF

Words and Music by
IRVING BERLIN

I sit a - lone _____ with a ta - ble and a chair, _____

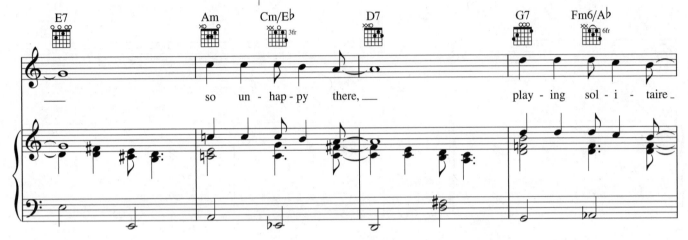

_____ so un - hap - py there, _____ play - ing sol - i - taire _____

_____ all by my - self. _____ I get lone -

- ly, _____ watch - ing the clock _____

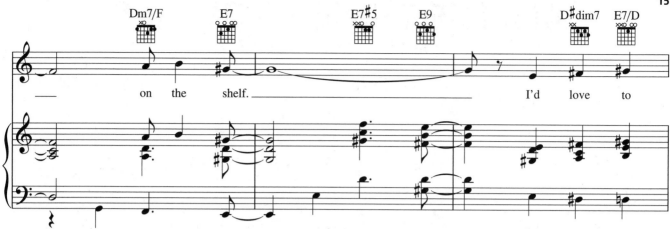

on the shelf. _____ I'd love to

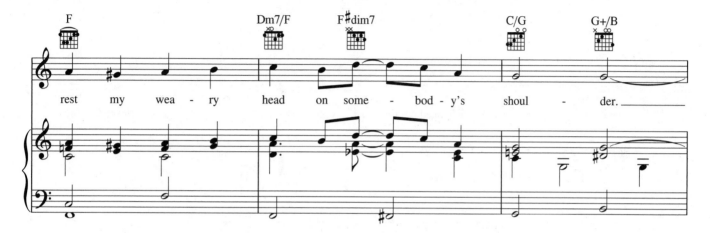

rest my wea - ry head on some - bod - y's shoul - der. _____

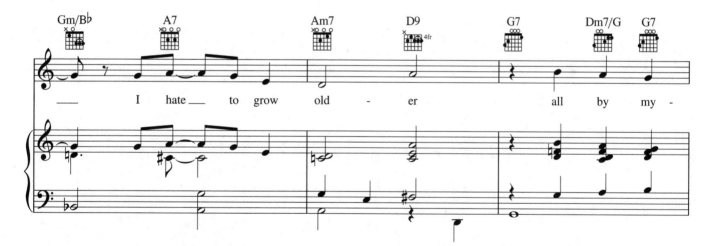

___ I hate ___ to grow old - er all by my -

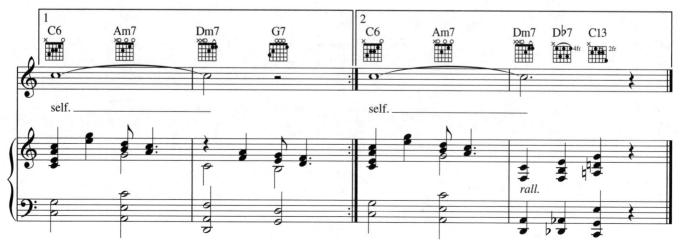

self. _____ self. _____

ALL THE THINGS YOU ARE

from VERY WARM FOR MAY

Lyrics by OSCAR HAMMERSTEIN II
Music by JEROME KERN

Time and a- gain I've longed for ad - ven - ture, some-thing to make my

heart beat the fast - er. What did I long for? I nev - er real - ly

knew. Find -ing your love, I've found my ad - ven - ture;

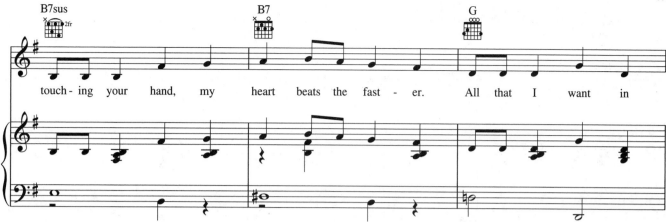

touch-ing your hand, my heart beats the fast - er. All that I want in

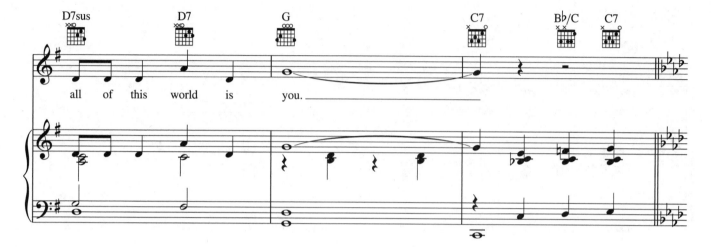

all of this world is you. ____

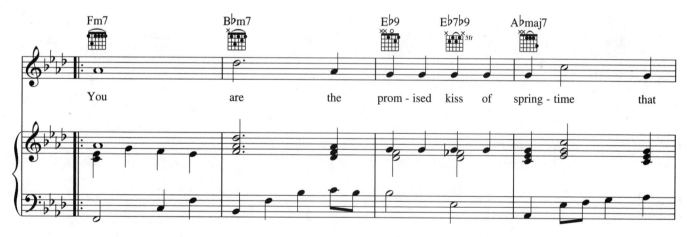

You are the prom-ised kiss of spring-time that

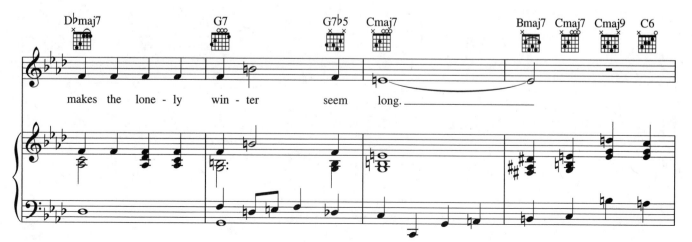

makes the lone-ly win-ter seem long. ____

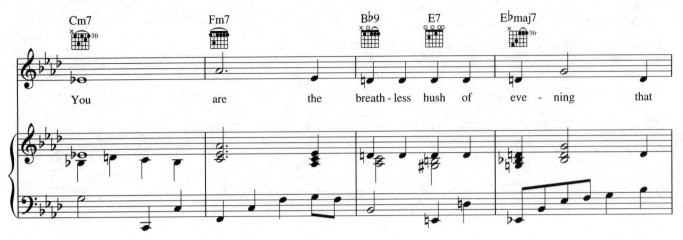

You are the breath-less hush of eve-ning that

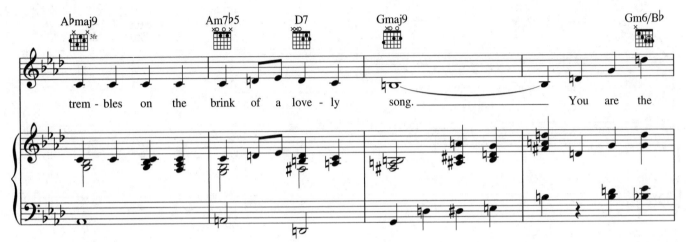

trem-bles on the brink of a love-ly song. _____ You are the

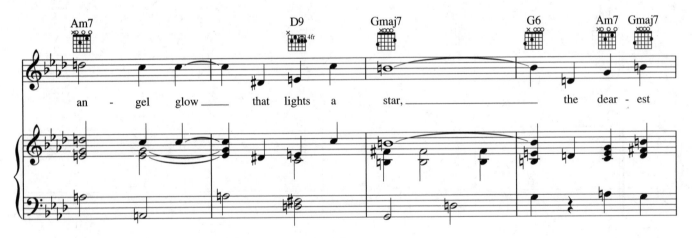

an-gel glow _____ that lights a star, _____ the dear-est

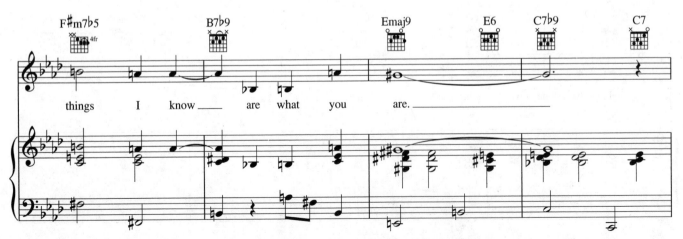

things I know _____ are what you are. _____

APRIL IN PARIS

Words by E.Y. "YIP" HARBURG
Music by VERNON DUKE

heart could sing, nev-er missed a warm em-brace, till

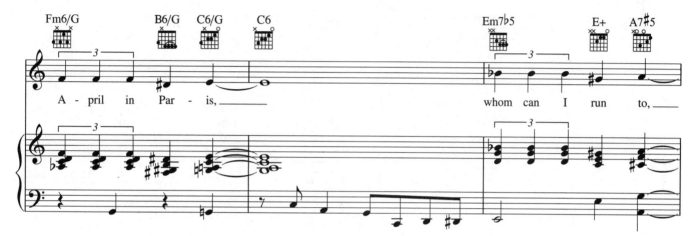

A - pril in Par - is, _____ whom can I run to, ____

what have you done to _____ my

heart?   heart? _____

AUTUMN LEAVES

English lyric by JOHNNY MERCER
French lyric by JACQUES PREVERT
Music by JOSEPH KOSMA

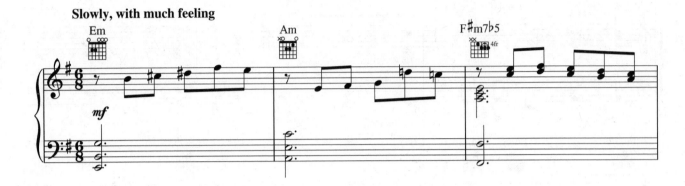

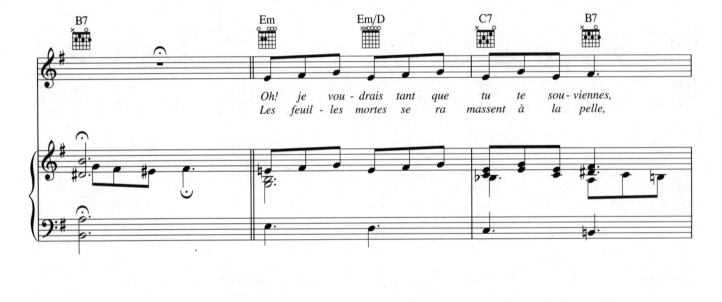

Oh! je vou - drais tant que tu te sou - viennes,
Les feuil - les mortes se ra massent à la pelle,

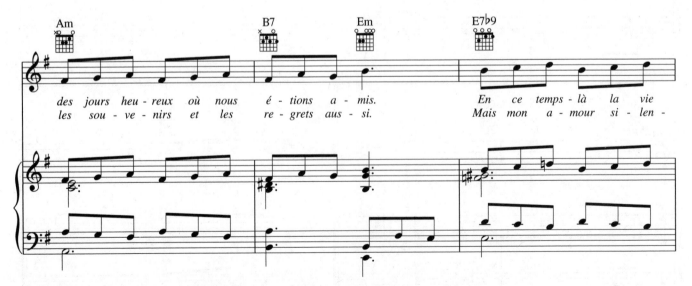

des jours heu - reux où nous é - tions a - mis.
les sou - ve - nirs et les re - grets aus - si.

En ce temps - là la vie
Mais mon a - mour si - len -

BEYOND THE SEA

By ALBERT LASRY and CHARLES TRENET
English Lyrics by JACK LAWRENCE

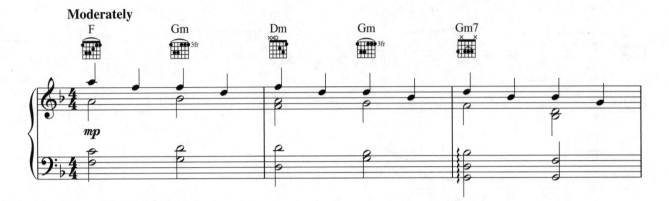

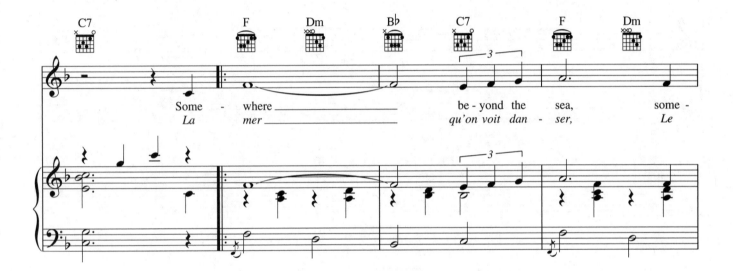

Some - where _____ be - yond the sea, some -
La mer _____ qu'on voit dan - ser, Le

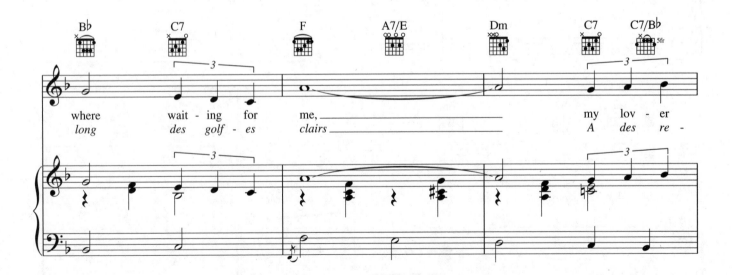

where wait - ing for me, _____ my lov - er
long des golf - es clairs _____ A des re -

THE BIRTH OF THE BLUES

Words by B.G. DeSYLVA and LEW BROWN
Music by RAY HENDERSON

breeze in the trees _____ sing-ing weird _____ mel - o - dies_

_____ and they made _____ that _____ the start _ of the

blues. _____ And from a jail came the wail_

_____ of a down - heart-ed frail, _____ and they played_

that as part — of the blues.

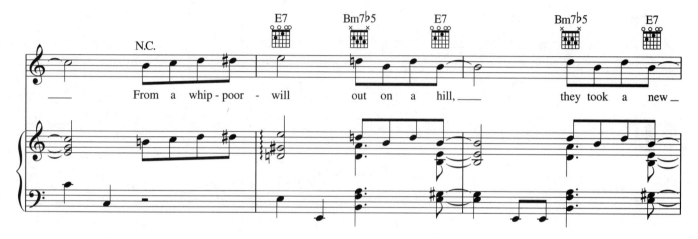

From a whip-poor-will out on a hill, ___ they took a new —

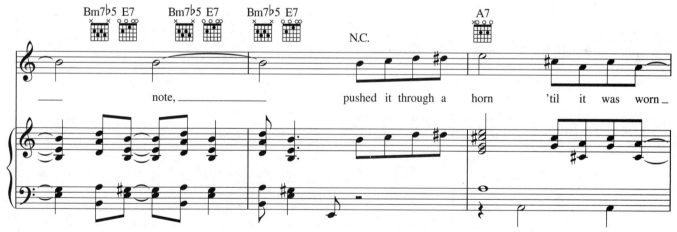

note, ___ pushed it through a horn 'til it was worn —

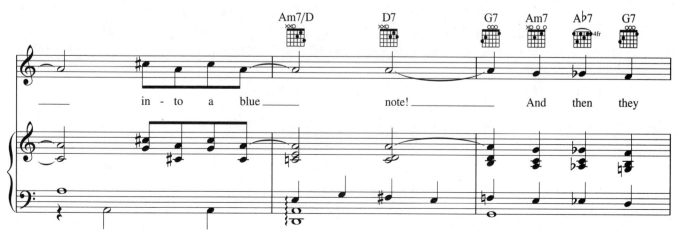

in-to a blue ___ note! ___ And then they

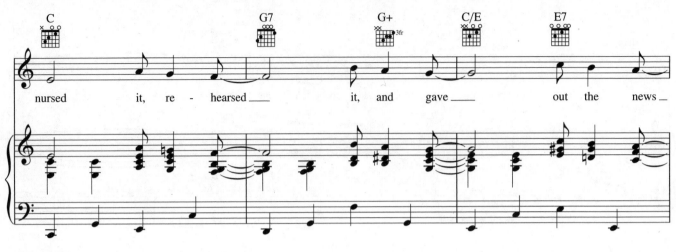

nursed it, re - hearsed it, and gave out the news

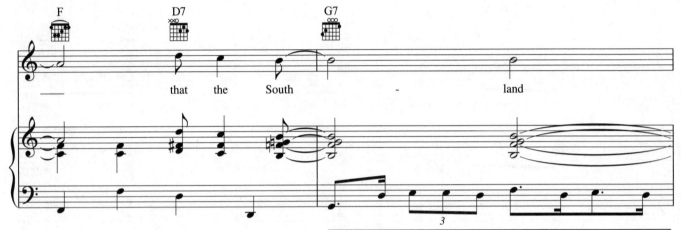

that the South - land

gave birth to the blues! _____

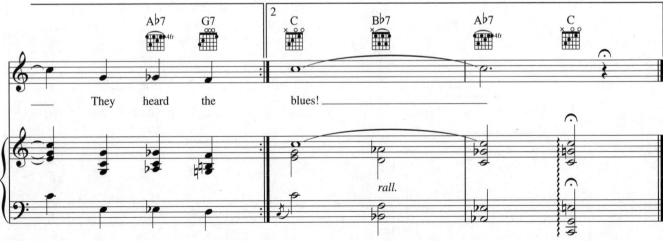

They heard the blues! _____

rall.

CHEEK TO CHEEK
from the RKO Radio Motion Picture TOP HAT

Words and Music by
IRVING BERLIN

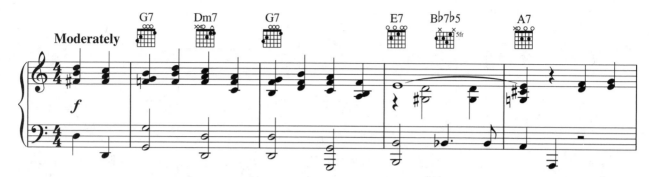

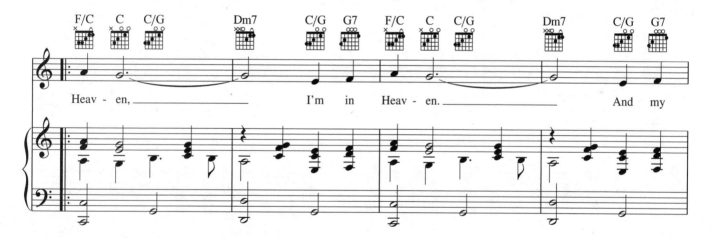

Heav - en, _____ I'm in Heav - en. _____ And my

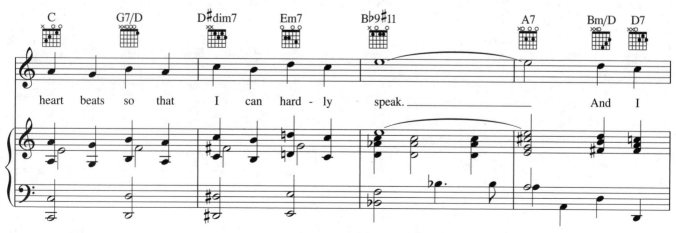

heart beats so that I can hard - ly speak. _____ And I

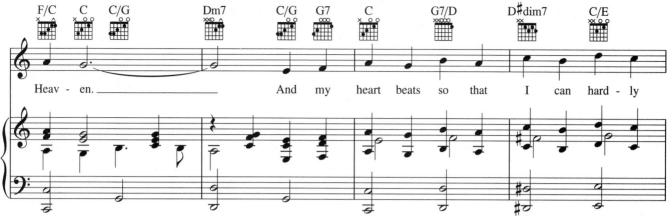

Heav - en. _____ And my heart beats so that I can hard - ly

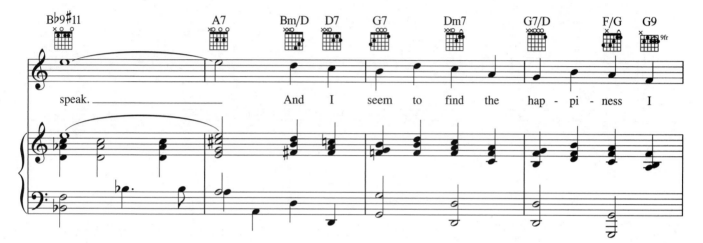

speak. _____ And I seem to find the hap - pi - ness I

seek _____ when we're out to - geth - er danc - ing cheek __ to cheek. __

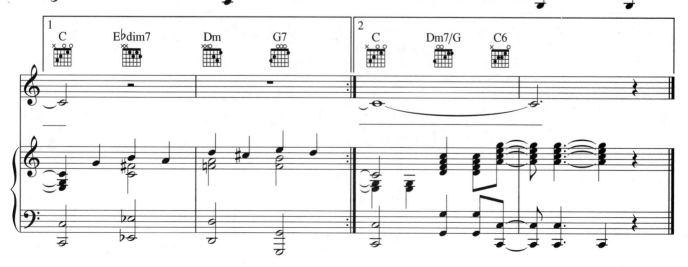

THE BLUE ROOM

from THE GIRL FRIEND

Words by LORENZ HART
Music by RICHARD RODGERS

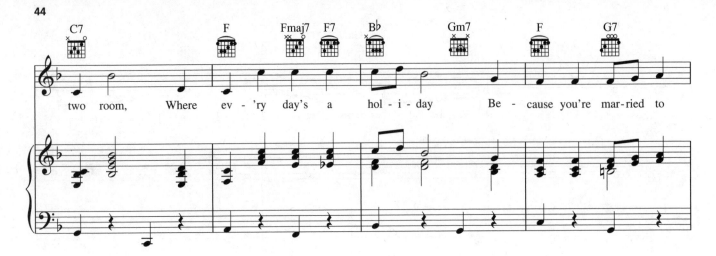

two room, Where ev - 'ry day's a hol - i - day Be - cause you're mar - ried to

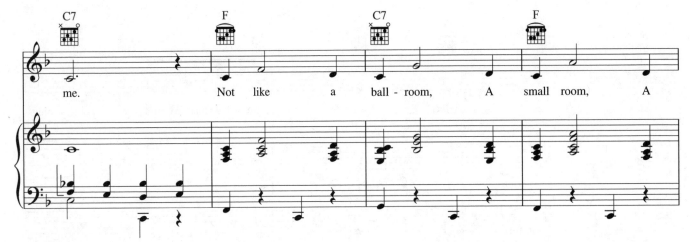

me. Not like a ball - room, A small room, A

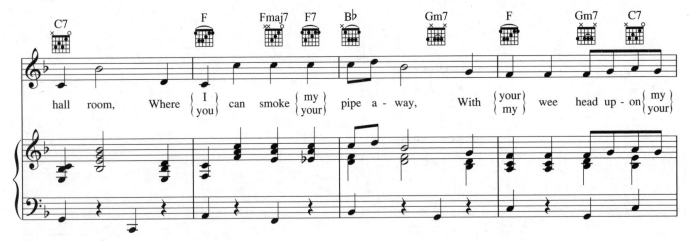

hall room, Where {I / you} can smoke {my / your} pipe a - way, With {your / my} wee head up - on {my / your}

knee. We will thrive on, keep a - live on Just noth - ing but

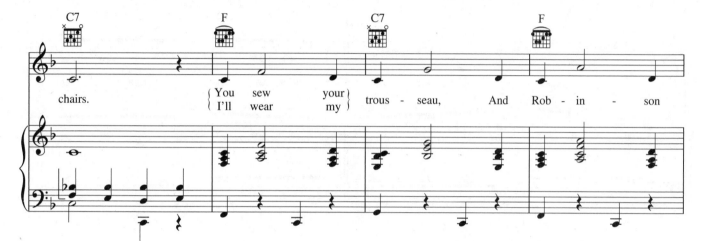

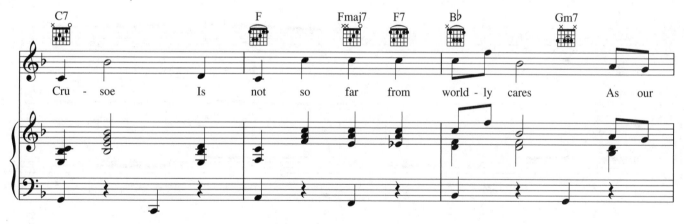

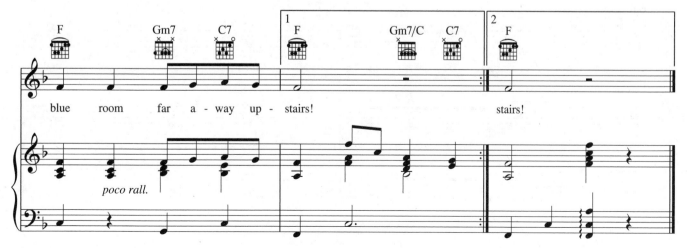

BOOGIE WOOGIE BUGLE BOY

from BUCK PRIVATES

Words and Music by DON RAYE
and HUGHIE PRINCE

Medium Boogie Woogie

He was a fa-mous trum-pet man from out Chi-ca-go way, ___ he had a "boo-gie" style that no one else could play. ___ He was the top man of his craft, ___

BYE BYE BLACKBIRD

from PETE KELLY'S BLUES

Lyric by MORT DIXON
Music by RAY HENDERSON

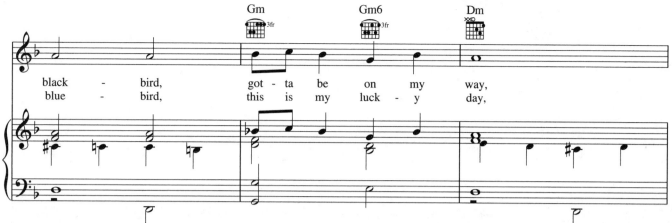

black - bird, gotta be on my way,
blue - bird, this is my luck - y day,

where there's sun - shine ga - lore.
now my dreams will ga come true.

Pack up all my care and woe,

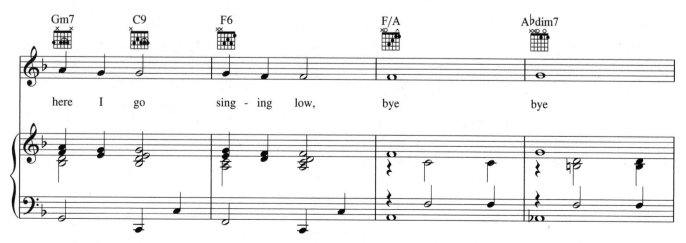

here I go sing - ing low, bye bye

Lyrics:

black - bird. _____ Where some-bod - y

waits for me, sug - ar's sweet, so is she,

bye bye black - bird. _____

No one here can love and un - der - stand me.

Oh, what hard luck sto - ries they all hand me;

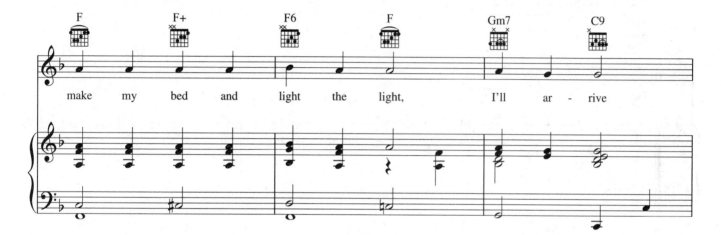

make my bed and light the light, I'll ar - rive

late to - night, black - bird _____ bye

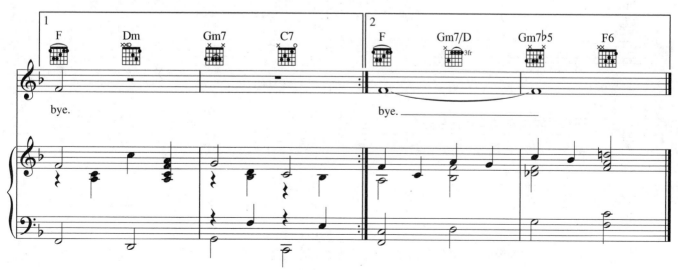

1. bye.

2. bye. _____

DAY BY DAY

Theme from the Paramount Television Series DAY BY DAY

Words and Music by SAMMY CAHN,
AXEL STORDAHL and PAUL WESTON

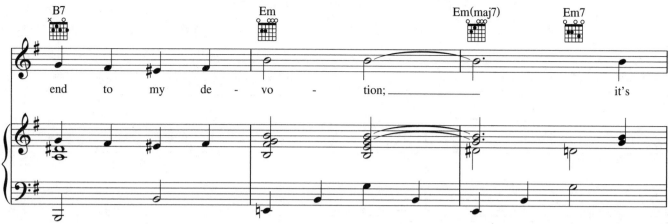

end to my de-vo-tion; _____ it's

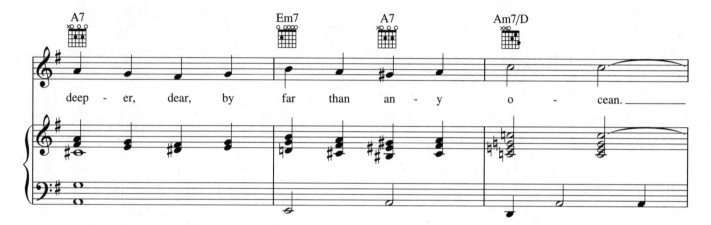

deep-er, dear, by far than an-y o-cean. _____

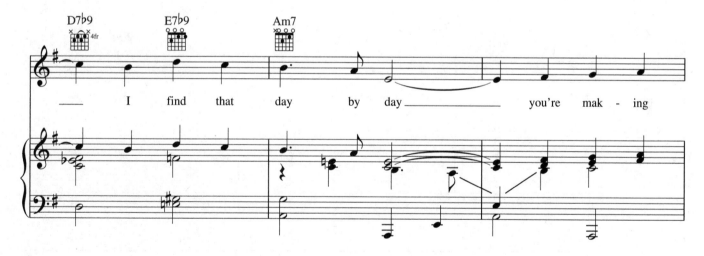

_____ I find that day by day _____ you're mak-ing

all my dreams come true. So come what may _____

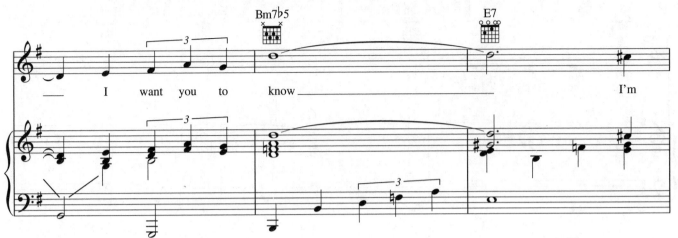

I want you to know _____ I'm

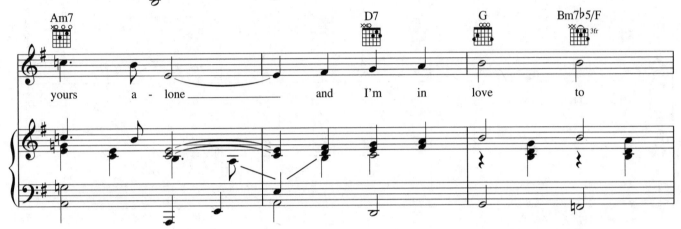

yours a - lone _____ and I'm in love to

stay, as we go through the years, day by

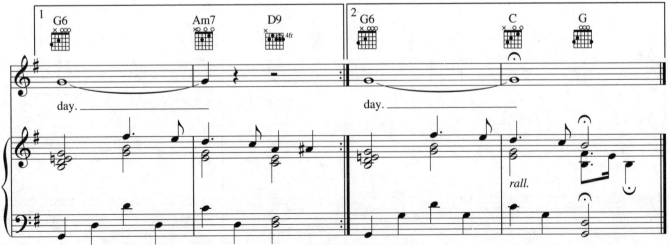

day. _____ day. _____

A DAY IN THE LIFE OF A FOOL
(Manhã de Carnaval)

Words by CARL SIGMAN
Music by LUIZ BONFA

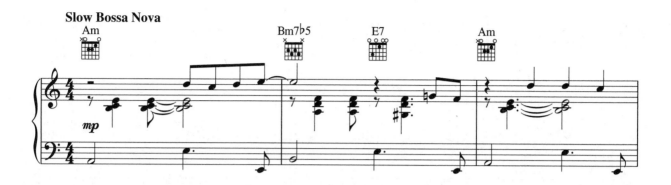

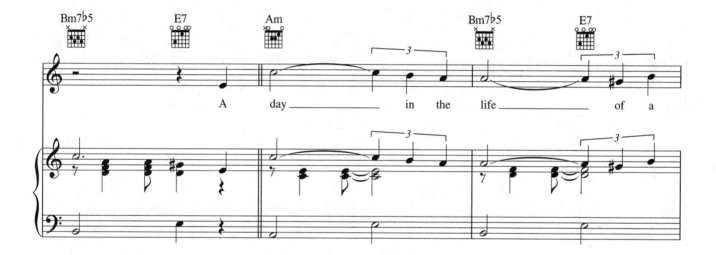

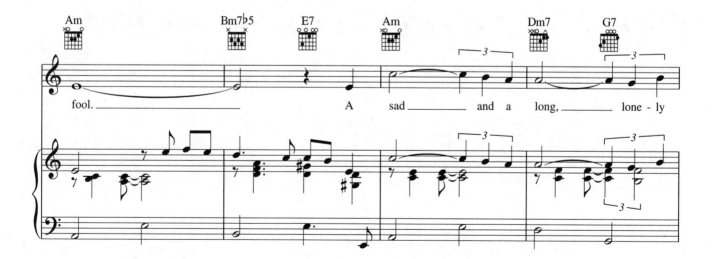

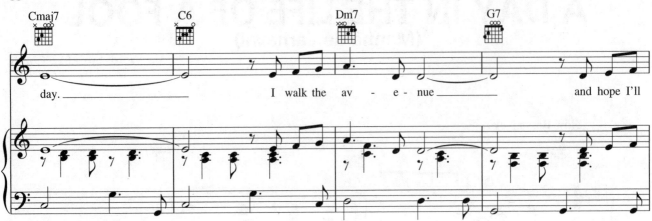

day. _____ I walk the av - e - nue _____ and hope I'll

run in - to _____ the wel-come sight of you _____ com - ing my

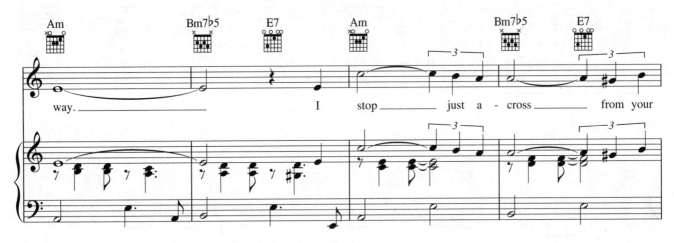

way. _____ I stop _____ just a - cross _____ from your

door, _____ but you're ____ nev - er home _____ an - y -

more. _____ So back to my room

and there in the gloom I cry _____ tears of good-

Rubato

bye. _____ 'Til you come back to me, that's the way it will be ev-'ry

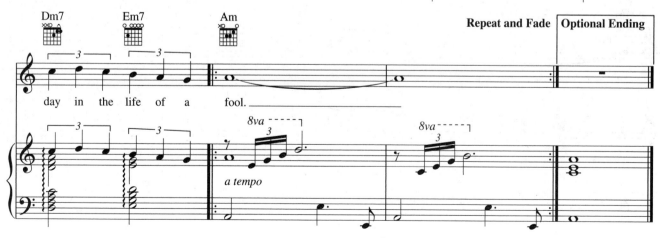

Repeat and Fade | Optional Ending

day in the life of a fool. _____

a tempo

DEARLY BELOVED

from YOU WERE NEVER LOVELIER

Music by JEROME KERN
Words by JOHNNY MERCER

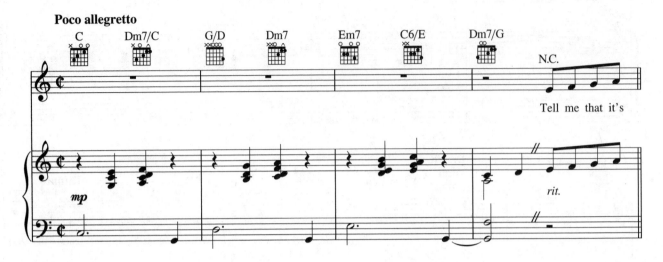

Tell me that it's true,

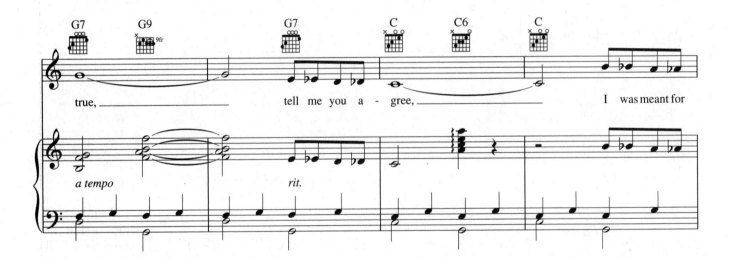

true, tell me you a-gree, I was meant for

you, you were meant for me.

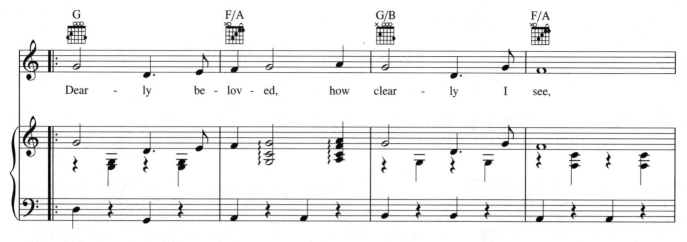

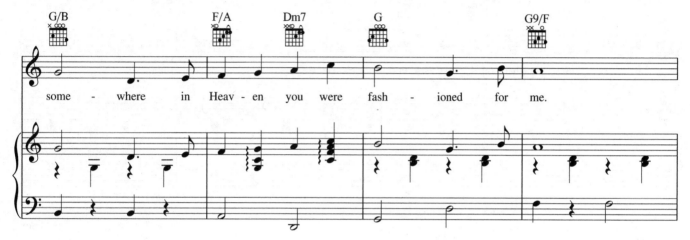

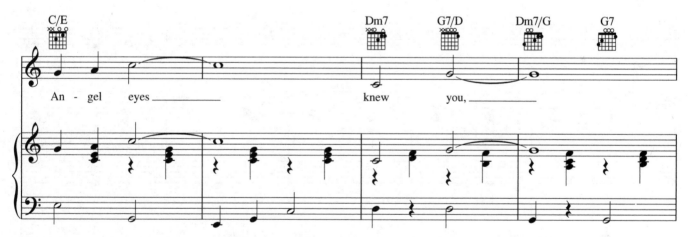

noth - ing could save me, fate gave me a sign.

I know that I'll be yours come show - er or shine;

so I say _____ mere - ly, _____ dear - ly be-

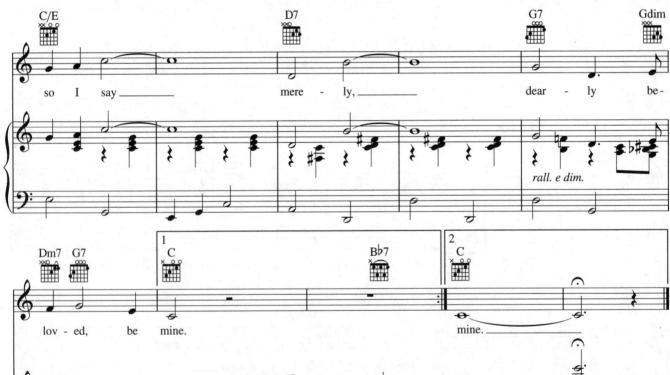

rall. e dim.

lov - ed, be mine.   mine. _____

a tempo

DON'T GET AROUND MUCH ANYMORE

from SOPHISTICATED LADY

Words and Music by DUKE ELLINGTON
and BOB RUSSELL

Missed the Sat - ur - day dance,

heard they crowd - ed the floor, could - n't bear it with - out

you, don't get a - round much an - y - more.

N.C. C
Thought I'd vis-it the club, got as far as the

A7 Am7 D7
door, they'd have ask'd me a-bout ___ you, ___

G7 C F
don't get a-round much an-y-more. Dar - ling, I guess ___

Fm7 Cmaj7 C7 C7#5 F
___ my mind's ___ more at ease, ___ but nev-er-the-less, ___

EAST OF THE SUN
(And West of the Moon)

Words and Music by
BROOKS BOWMAN

EASY TO LOVE
(You'd Be So Easy to Love)
from BORN TO DANCE

Words and Music by
COLE PORTER

Moderately

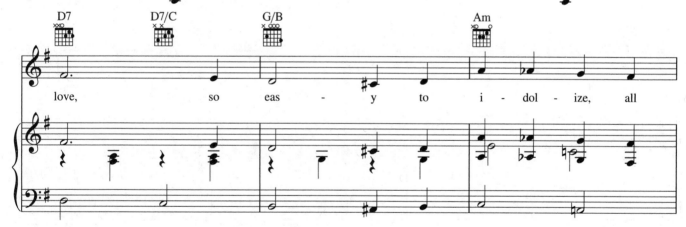

worth the yearn - ing for, _____

so swell to keep ev - 'ry home fire burn - ing for. _____

_____ We'd be so

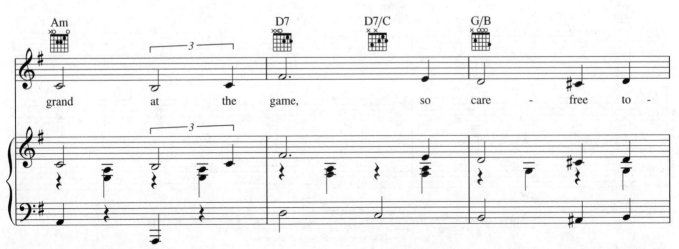

grand at the game, so care - free to -

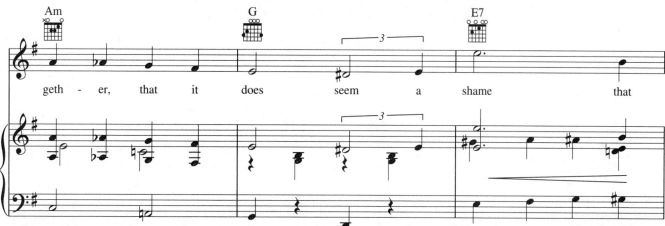

geth - er, that it does seem a shame that

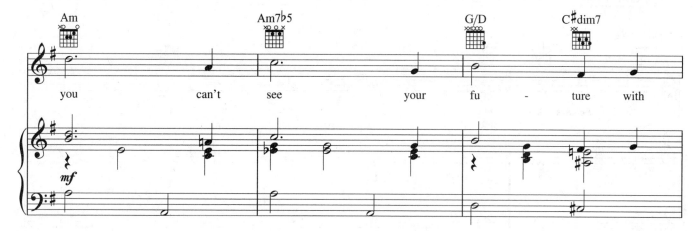

you can't see your fu - ture with

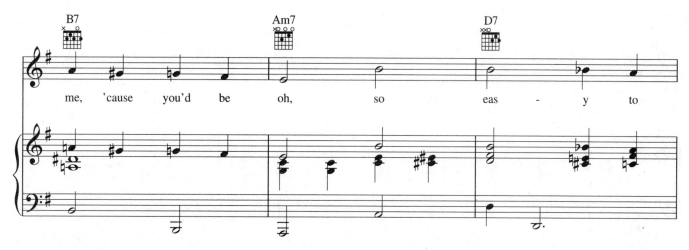

me, 'cause you'd be oh, so eas - y to

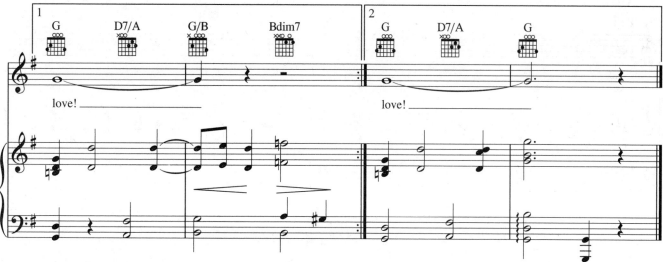

love! _____ love! _____

A FINE ROMANCE

from SWING TIME

Words by DOROTHY FIELDS
Music by JEROME KERN

Female: A fine ro-mance, with no
fine ro-mance, my good

kiss-es! A fine ro-mance, my
fel-low! You take ro-mance, I'll

friend, this is! We should be like a
take Jell - O! You're calm-er than the

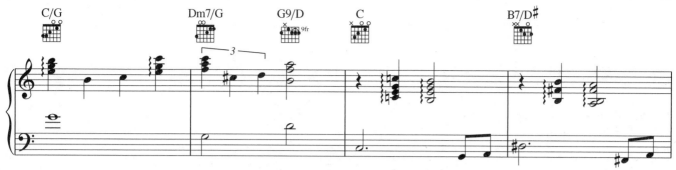

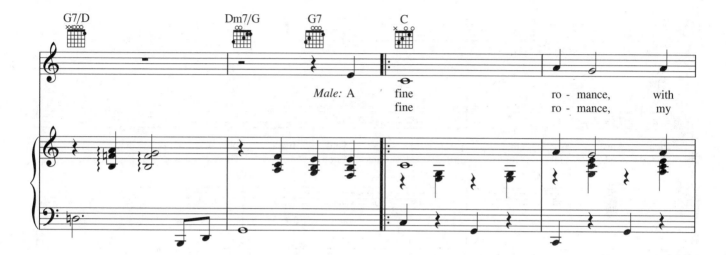

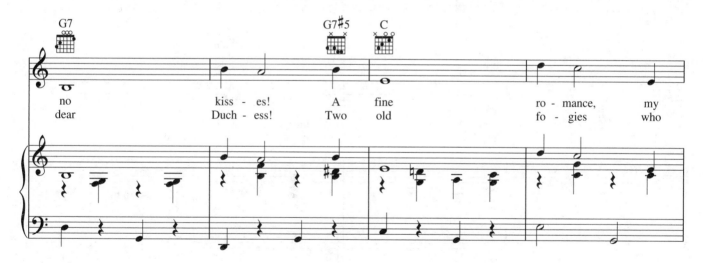

76

pinch - es! You're just as hard to land as the "Île de
wom - an! You nev - er give the or - chids I send a

France!" I have - n't got a chance.
glance. No! You like cac - tus plants.

This is a fine ro - mance!
This is a fine ro -

A mance!

(I Love You)
FOR SENTIMENTAL REASONS

Words by DEEK WATSON
Music by WILLIAM BEST

I love you _____ for sen - ti - men - tal

rea - sons. _____ I hope you do be - lieve me; _____

_____ I'll give you my heart. _____ I

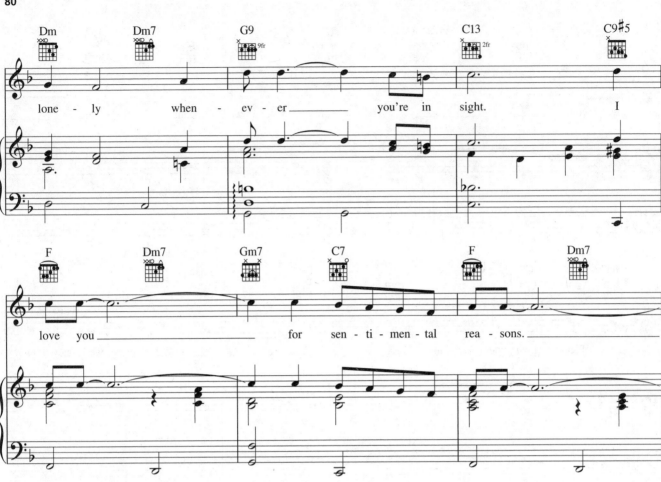

lone - ly when - ev - er _____ you're in sight. I

love you _____ for sen - ti - men - tal rea - sons. _____

____ I hope you do be - lieve me; _____ I've giv - en you my

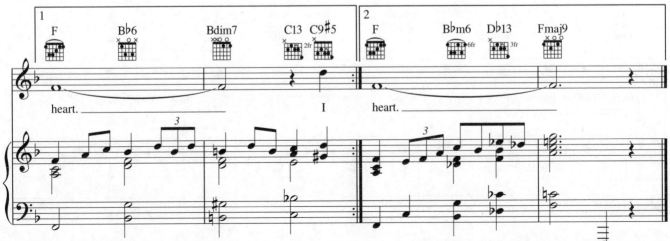

heart. _____ I

heart. _____

HAVE I TOLD YOU LATELY THAT I LOVE YOU

Words and Music by
SCOTT WISEMAN

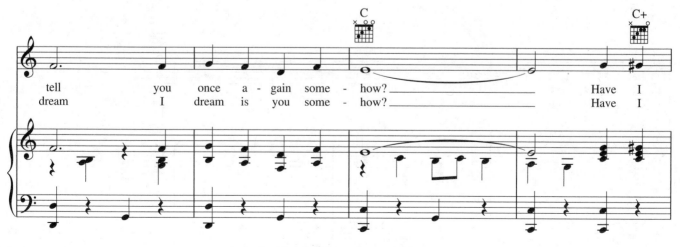

told / told with all / with you my / why heart / the and / nights soul / are how / long I / when a- / you're not

dore you? / with me? Well, dar - ling, I'm tell - ing you

now. (I'm tell-ing you, tell-ing you.) Have I now. (I'm tell-ing you.)

My heart would break in two if I should lose you.

FOR YOU, FOR ME, FOR EVERMORE

Music and Lyrics by GEORGE GERSHWIN
and IRA GERSHWIN

Moderately

Par-a-dise can-not re-

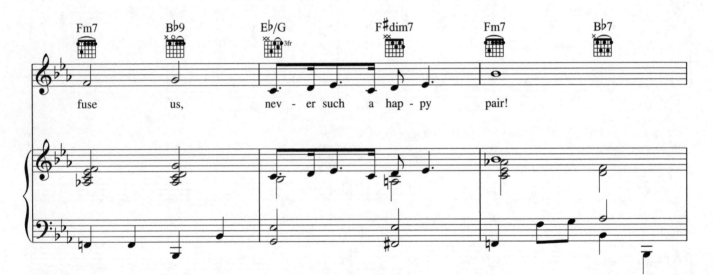

fuse us, nev-er such a hap-py pair!

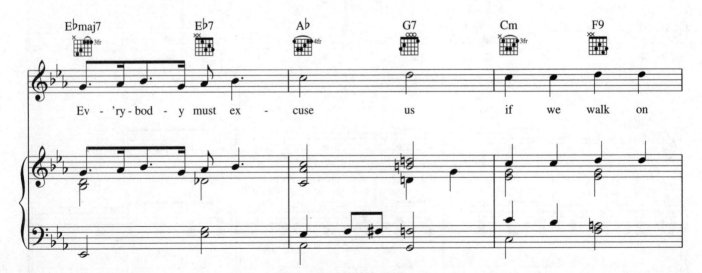

Ev-'ry-bod-y must ex-cuse us if we walk on

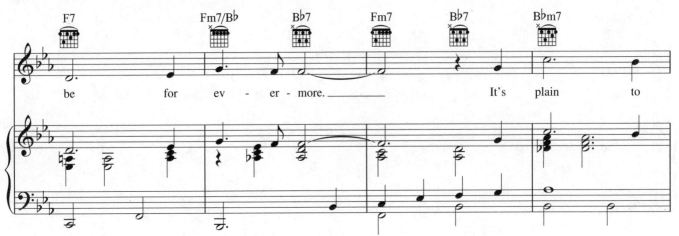

be for ev - er - more. _____ It's plain to

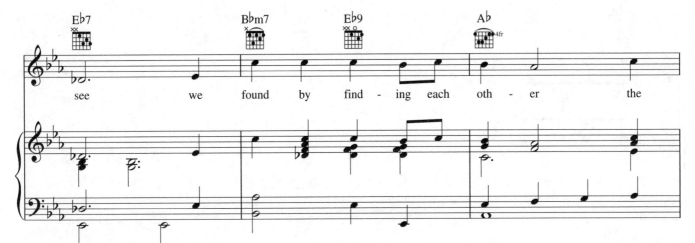

see we found by find - ing each oth - er the

love we wait - ed for. _____ I'm

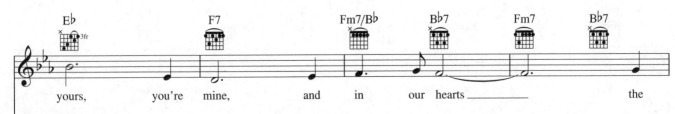

yours, you're mine, and in our hearts _____ the

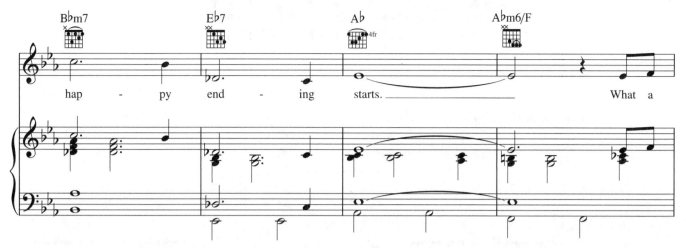

hap - py end - ing starts. _____ What a

love - ly world this world will be, with a world of love in

store for you, for me, for ev - er -

more! _____ For more! _____

THE GLORY OF LOVE

from GUESS WHO'S COMING TO DINNER

Words and Music by
BILLY HILL

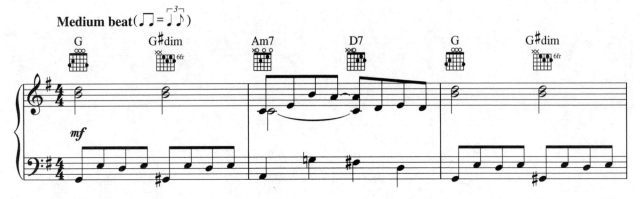

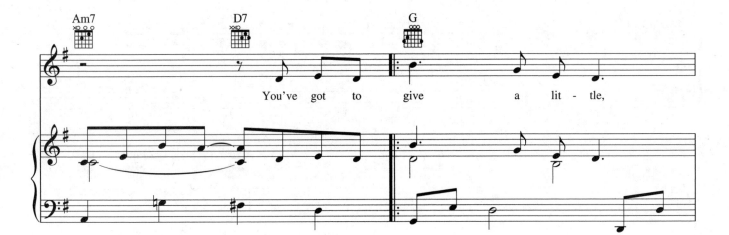

You've got to give a lit - tle,

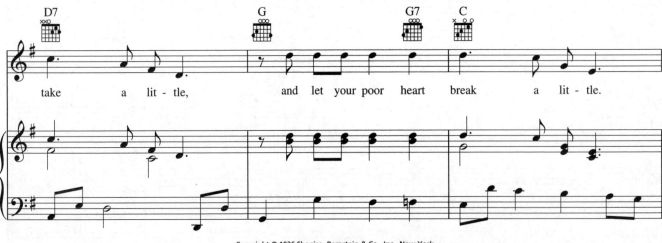

take a lit - tle, and let your poor heart break a lit - tle.

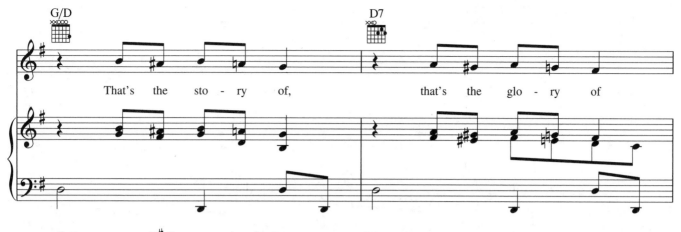

That's the sto - ry of, that's the glo - ry of

love. _____ You've got to laugh a lit - tle,

cry a lit - tle be - fore the clouds roll by a lit - tle.

That's the sto - ry of, that's the glo - ry of

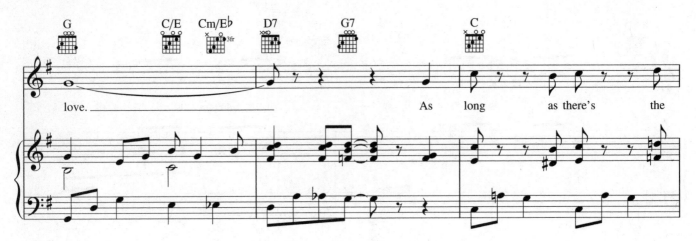

love. _____ As long as there's the

two of us, we've got the world and all its charms. _____ And

when the world is through with us,

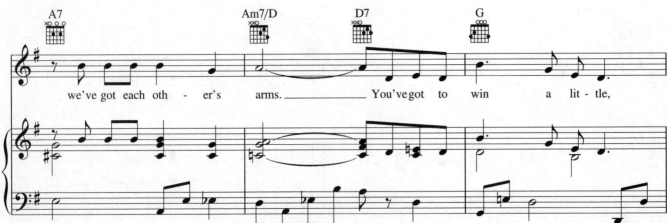

we've got each oth - er's arms. _____ You've got to win a lit - tle,

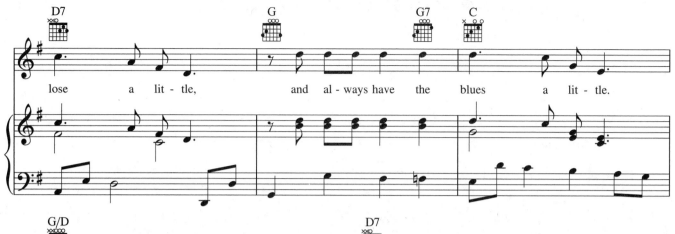

lose a lit-tle, and al-ways have the blues a lit-tle.

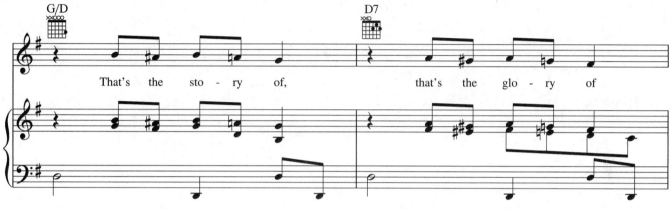

That's the sto-ry of, that's the glo-ry of

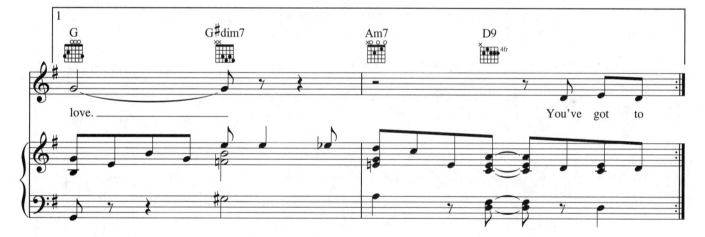

love. _____ You've got to

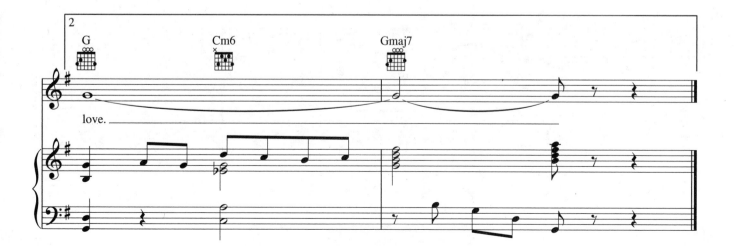

love. _____

GOODBYE TO LOVE

Words and Music by RICHARD CARPENTER
and JOHN BETTIS

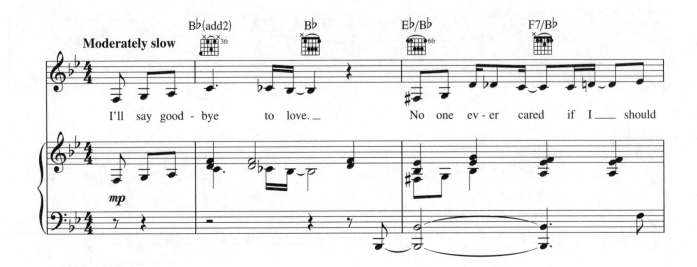

I'll say good-bye to love. No one ev-er cared if I should

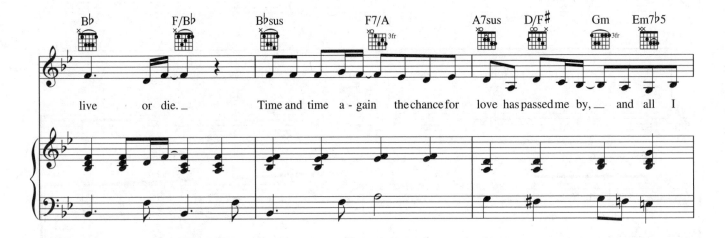

live or die. Time and time a-gain the chance for love has passed me by, and all I

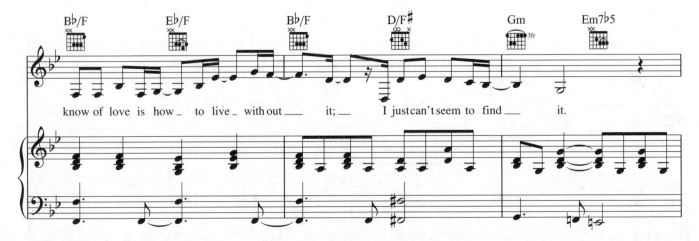

know of love is how to live with-out it; I just can't seem to find it.

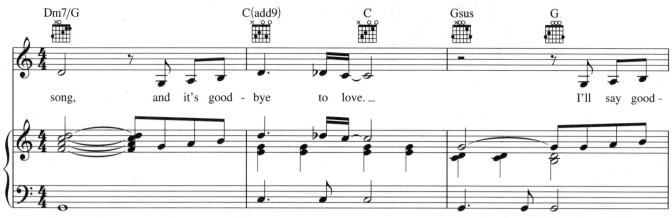

song, and it's good - bye to love. ___ I'll say good -

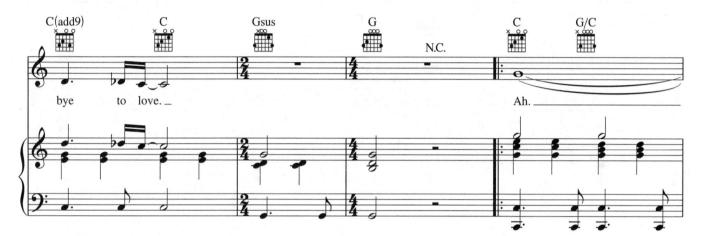

bye to love. ___ Ah. ___

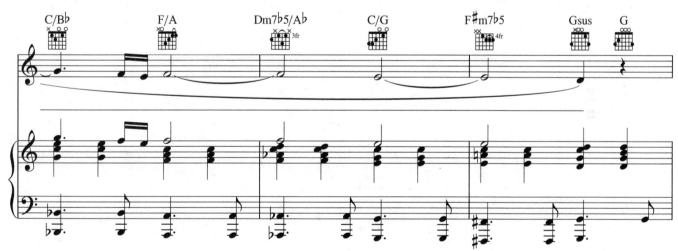

Repeat and Fade

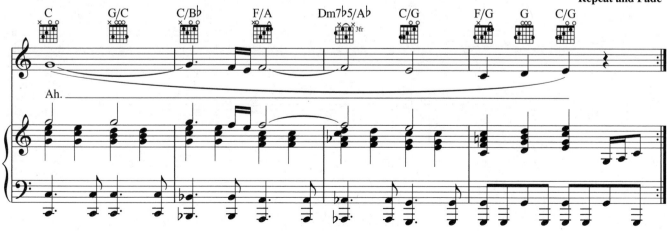

Ah. ___

HEART AND SOUL

from the Paramount Short Subject A SONG IS BORN

Words by FRANK LOESSER
Music by HOAGY CARMICHAEL

Moderately, lightly rhythmical

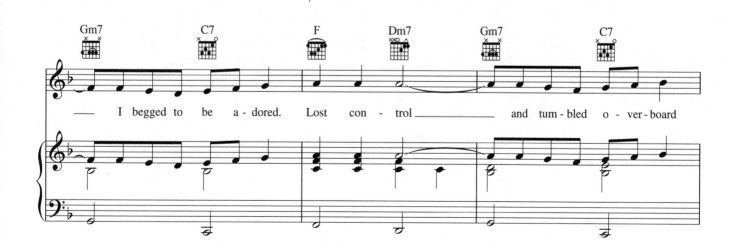

glad - ly _____ that mag - ic night we kissed there in the

moon - mist. Oh! but your lips were thrill - ing,

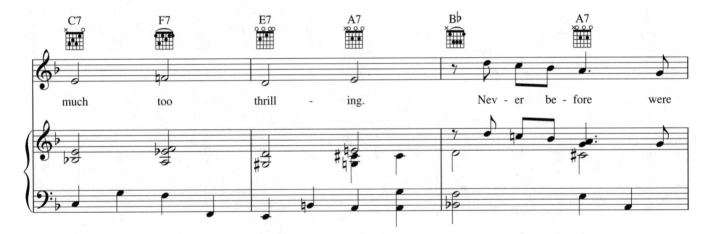

much too thrill - ing. Nev - er be - fore were

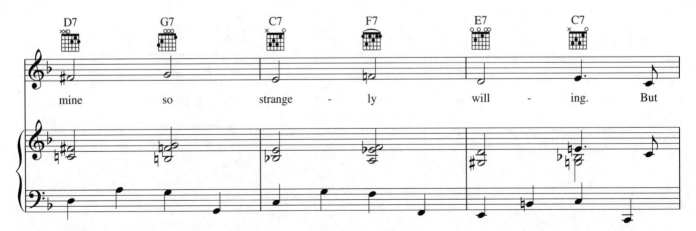

mine so strange - ly will - ing. But

now I see _____ what one em-brace can do. Look at me, _____

____ it's got me lov-ing you mad - ly; _____ that lit-tle kiss you

stole held all my heart and soul. _____

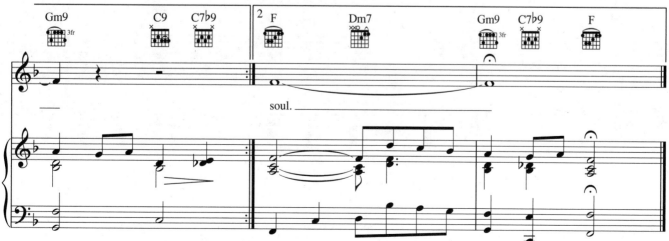

____ soul. _____

I GET ALONG WITHOUT YOU VERY WELL
(Except Sometimes)

Words and Music by HOAGY CARMICHAEL
Inspired by a poem written by J.B. THOMPSON

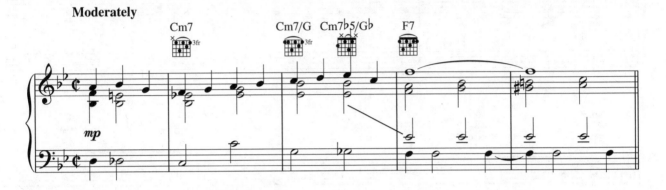

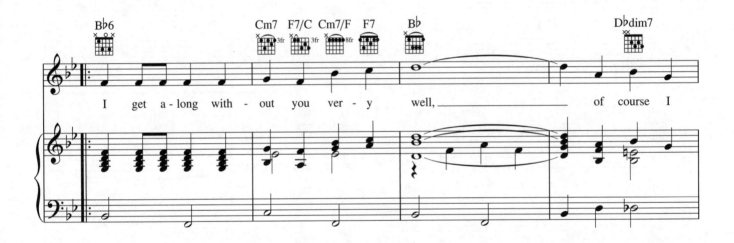

I get a-long with-out you ver-y well, _____ of course I

do; _____ ex-cept when soft rains fall _____ and drip from

leaves, then I re-call the thrill of be-ing shel-tered in your

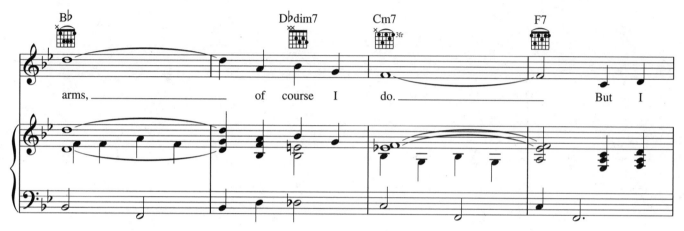

arms, _____ of course I do. _____ But I

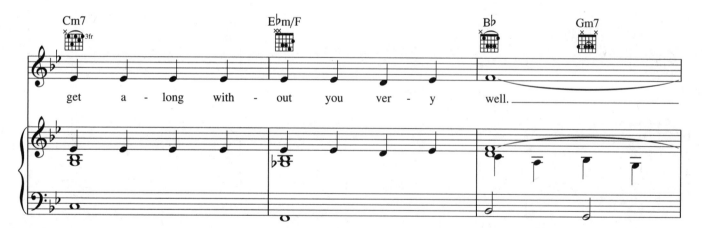

get a-long with-out you ver-y well. _____

____ I've for-got-ten you, just like I

should, _____ of course I have; _____

____ ex - cept to hear your name _____ or some - one's

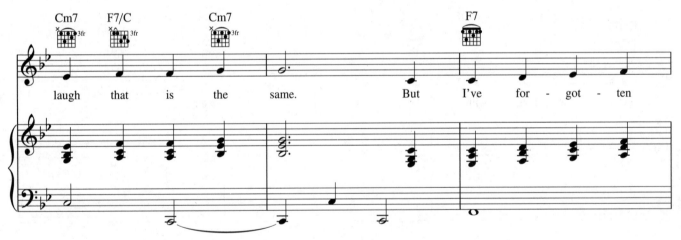

laugh that is the same. But I've for - got - ten

you just like I should, _____ what a guy! _____

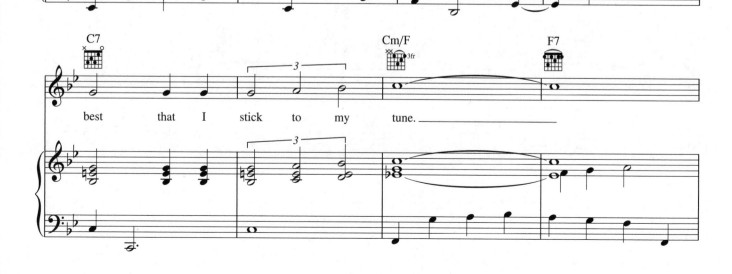

I LEFT MY HEART IN SAN FRANCISCO

Words by DOUGLASS CROSS
Music by GEORGE CORY

I LOVE PARIS

from CAN-CAN
from HIGH SOCIETY

Words and Music by
COLE PORTER

I love Par - is in the win - ter when it driz - zles,

I love Par - is in the sum - mer when it siz - zles.

I love Par - is ev - 'ry mo - ment, _____

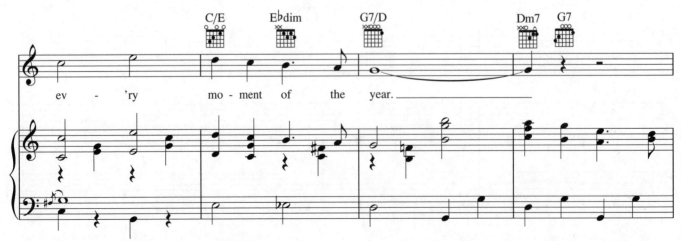

ev - 'ry mo - ment of the year. _____

I REMEMBER YOU

from the Paramount Picture THE FLEET'S IN

Words by JOHNNY MERCER
Music by VICTOR SCHERTZINGER

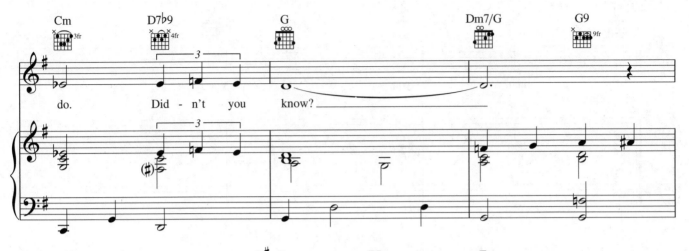

do. Did -n't you know?_____

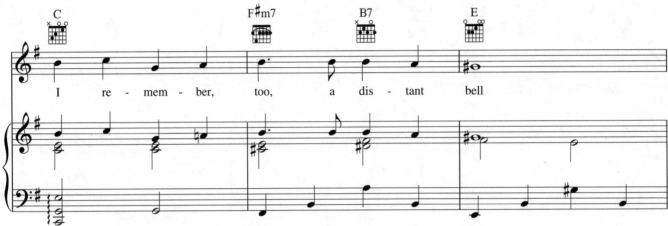

I re - mem - ber, too, a dis - tant bell

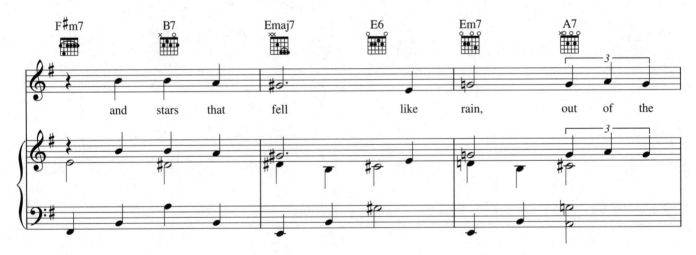

and stars that fell like rain, out of the

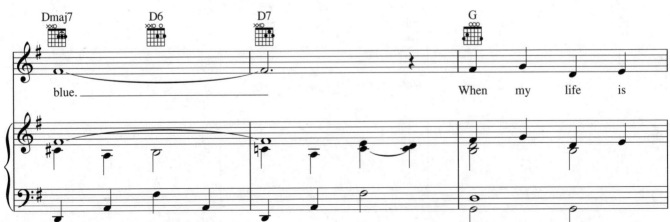

blue._____ When my life is

I WILL WAIT FOR YOU
from THE UMBRELLAS OF CHERBOURG

Music by MICHEL LEGRAND
Original French Text by JACQUES DEMY
English Words by NORMAN GIMBEL

you; for a thou - sand sum - mers I will

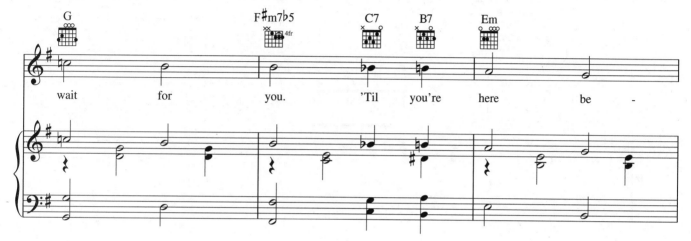

wait for you. 'Til you're here be -

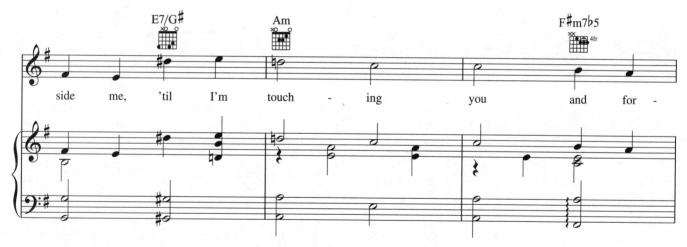

side me, 'til I'm touch - ing you and for -

ev - er - more shar - ing your love.

I WISH I DIDN'T LOVE YOU SO

from the Paramount Picture THE PERILS OF PAULINE

Words and Music by
FRANK LOESSER

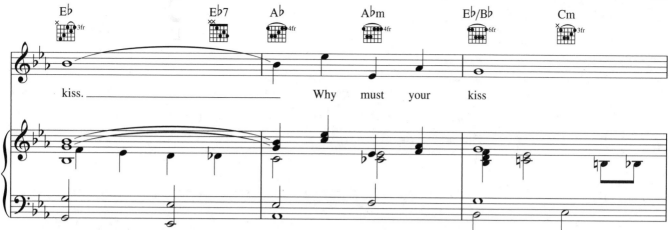

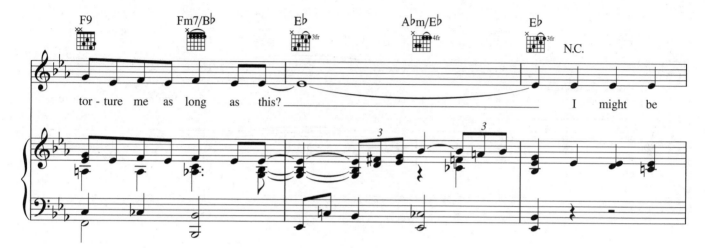

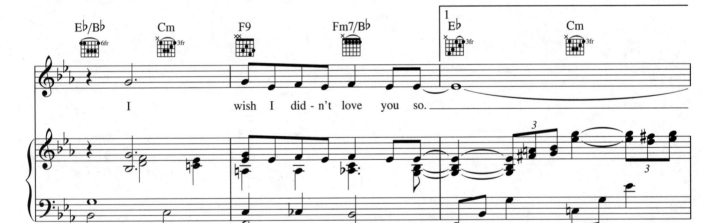

I'LL NEVER SMILE AGAIN

Words and Music by
RUTH LOWE

I WISH YOU LOVE

English Words by ALBERT BEACH
French Words and Music by CHARLES TRENET

day, but be-fore you walk a - way,

I sin-cere-ly want to say: I wish you

blue - birds in the spring, to give your heart a song to sing, and then a

kiss, but more than this, I wish you love. And in Ju-

ly, a lem-on-ade, to cool you in some leaf-y

glade. I wish you health and more than wealth, I wish you

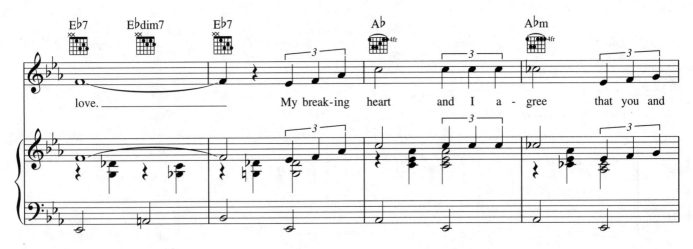

love. _____ My break-ing heart and I a-gree that you and

I could nev-er be, so with my best, my ver-y

I WON'T DANCE

from ROBERTA

Words and Music by JIMMY McHUGH, DOROTHY FIELDS,
JEROME KERN, OSCAR HAMMERSTEIN II
and OTTO HARBACH

Think of what you're los-ing by con-stant-ly re-fus-ing to dance with me.

____ You'd be the i-dol of France with me! ____ And yet you stand there and

shake your fool-ish head dra-mat-i-c'lly. While I wait here

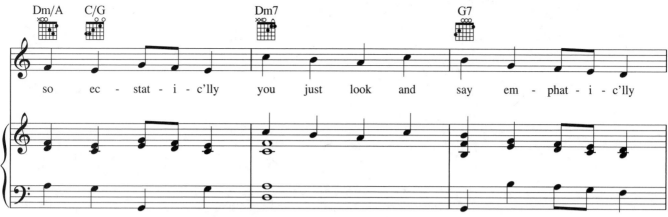

so ec - stat - i - c'lly you just look and say em - phat - i - c'lly

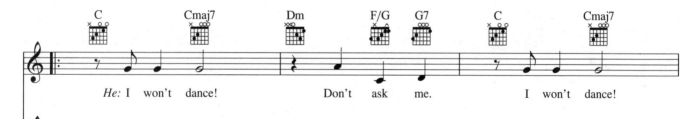

not this sea - son! There's a rea - son!

He: I won't dance! Don't ask me. I won't dance!

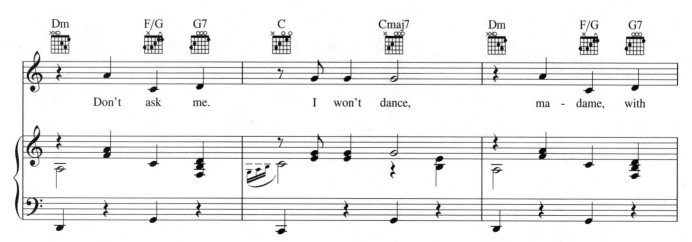

Don't ask me. I won't dance, ma - dame, with

you. _____ My heart won't let my feet do things they should do! __

You know what?

You're love - ly. *She:* And so what? I'm love - ly! *He:* But oh! What

you do to me! _____ I'm like an o - cean wave that's

nen - tal." _____ *He:* But this feel - ing

is - n't pure - ly men - tal. _____ For heav - en

rest us, _____ I'm not as - bes - tos. _____

___ And that's why I won't dance! Why should I?

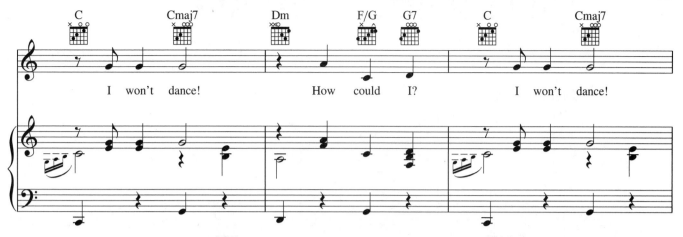

I'LL REMEMBER APRIL

Words and Music by PAT JOHNSON,
DON RAYE and GENE DE PAUL

Moderately, with expression

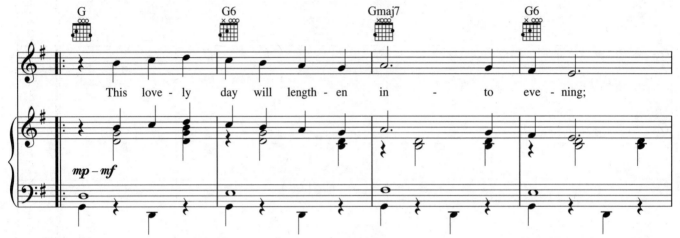

This love-ly day will length-en in-to eve-ning;

we'll sigh good-bye to all we've ev-er had. _____ A-

lone, where we have walked to-geth-er, _____ I'll re-

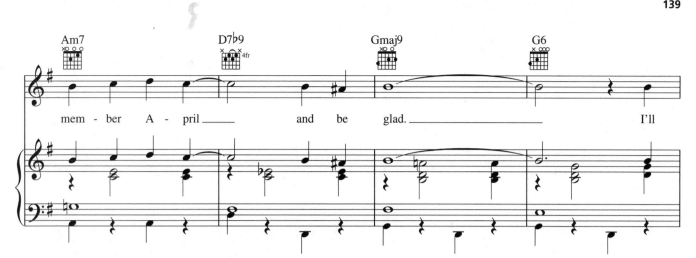

member A - pril _____ and be glad. _____ I'll

be con - tent _____ you loved me once in A - pril. Your

lips were warm _____ and love and spring were new. _____

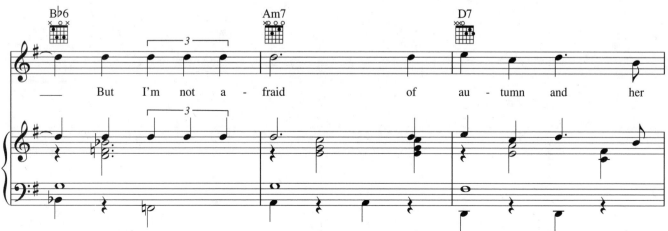

_____ But I'm not a - fraid of au - tumn and her

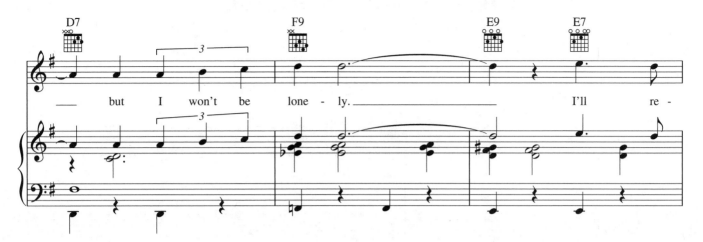

but I won't be lone-ly. _____ I'll re-

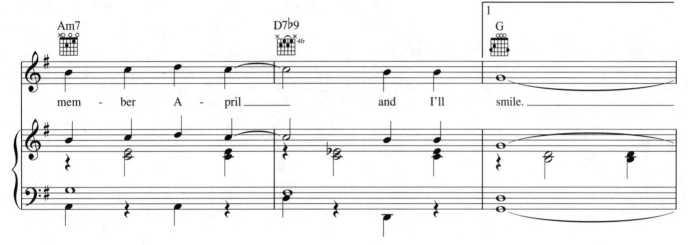

mem-ber A-pril _____ and I'll smile. _____

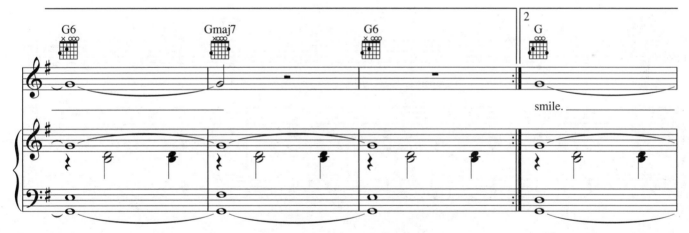

smile. _____

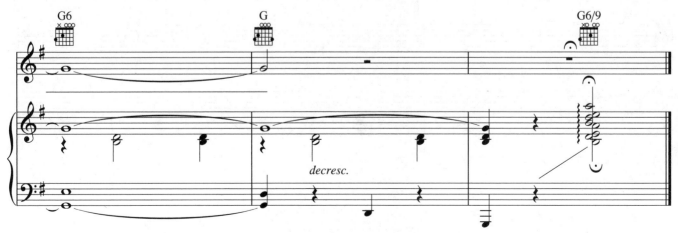

decresc.

I'M OLD FASHIONED

from YOU WERE NEVER LOVELIER

Words by JOHNNY MERCER
Music by JEROME KERN

not that I ev-er try to be a saint, _____

I'm the type that they clas-si-fy as quaint. _____

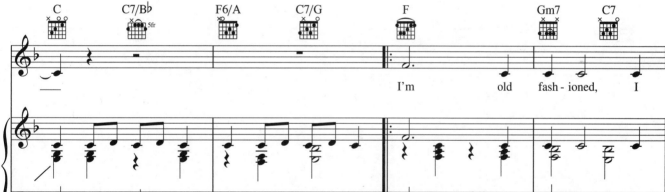

I'm old fash-ioned, I

love the moon-light, I love the old fash-ioned

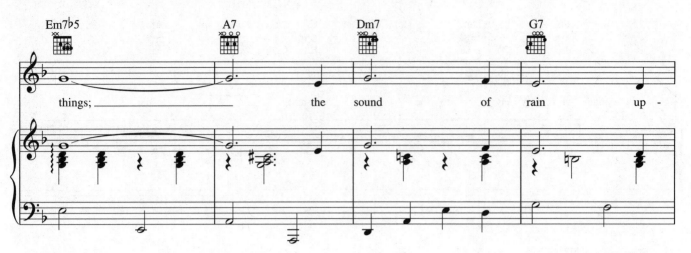

things; _____ the sound of rain up -

on a win - dow - pane, the star - ry song that A - pril

sings. _____ This year's fan - cies are

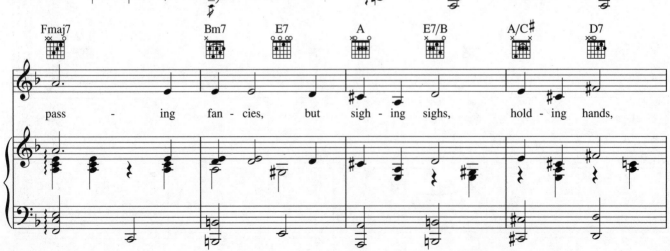

pass - ing fan - cies, but sigh - ing sighs, hold - ing hands,

I'VE GOT THE WORLD ON A STRING

Lyric by TED KOEHLER
Music by HAROLD ARLEN

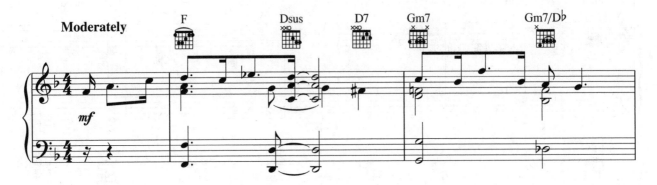

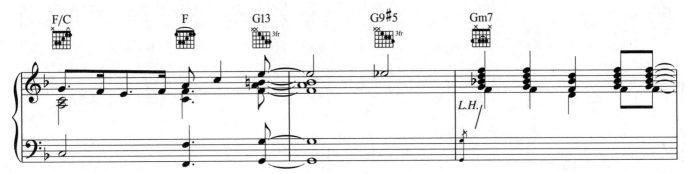

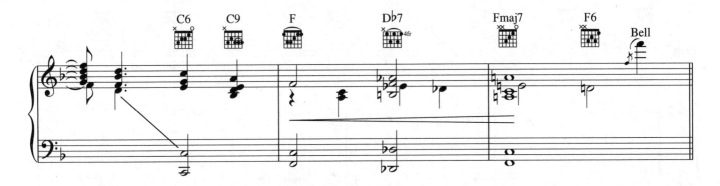

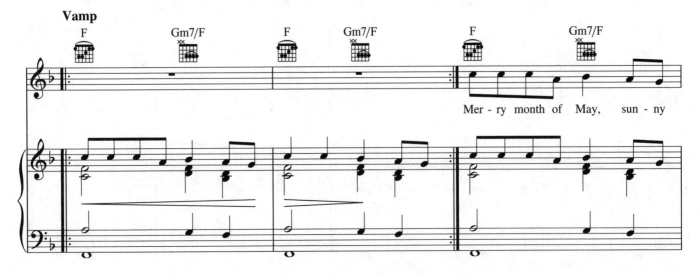

Mer - ry month of May, sun - ny

skies of blue, clouds have rolled a - way and the sun peeps thru, May ex -

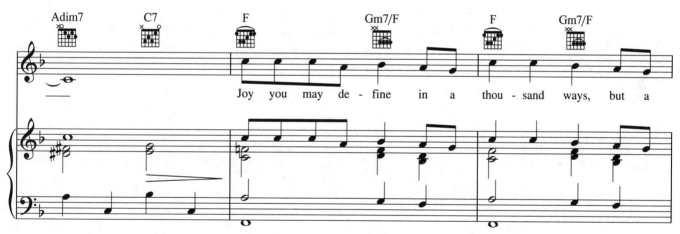

press _____ hap - pi - ness, _____

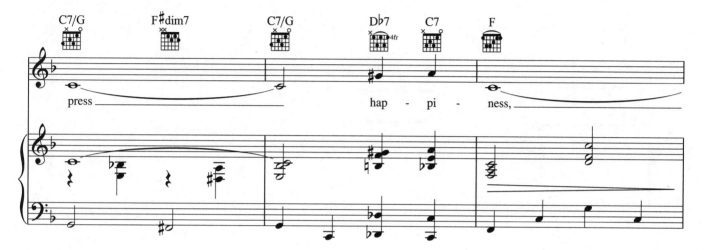

Joy you may de - fine in a thou - sand ways, but a

case like mine needs a "spe - cial phrase" to re - veal _____

how I feel. _____ I've got the

world on a string, _ sit - tin' on a rain - bow, Got the string a - round my fin -

- ger, what a world, what a _____ life, I'm in

love! I've got a song that I sing, _

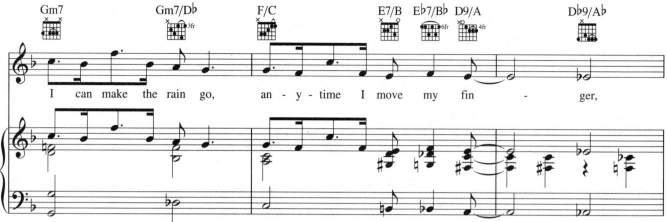

I can make the rain go, an-y-time I move my fin - ger,

Luck - y me, can't you ___ see, I'm in love. ___

___ Life is a beau - ti-ful thing, ___ as long as I hold the string, ___

I'd be a sil - ly so and so,

if I should ev-er let go, _____ I've got the

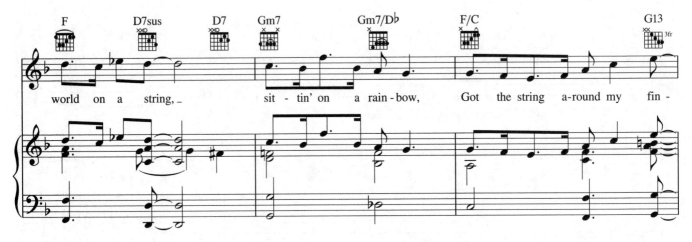

world on a string, _ sit-tin' on a rain-bow, Got the string a-round my fin-

- ger, what a world, what a _____ life, I'm in

love! _____ I've got the love! _____

I'VE GOT YOU UNDER MY SKIN

from BORN TO DANCE

Words and Music by
COLE PORTER

sake of hav-ing you near, in spite of a warn-ing voice that comes in the night and re-

peats and re-peats in my ear: _____ "Don't you know, lit-tle fool, _____

_____ you nev-er can win. _____ Use your men-tal - i - ty, _____

_____ wake up to re-al - i - ty." _____ But each

time I do, just the thought of you makes me stop be-fore I be-

rit.

gin, 'cause I've got you _____ un-der my

a tempo

skin. _____ I've ___

poco rall.

8vb

IN THE STILL OF THE NIGHT

from ROSALIE
from NIGHT AND DAY

Words and Music by
COLE PORTER

In the still of the night, ____

As I gaze from my win - dow,

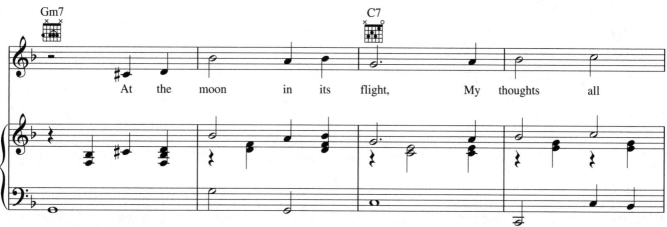

At the moon in its flight, My thoughts all

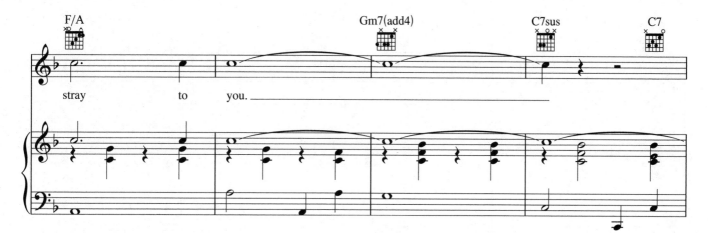

stray to you. _____

In the still of the night, _____

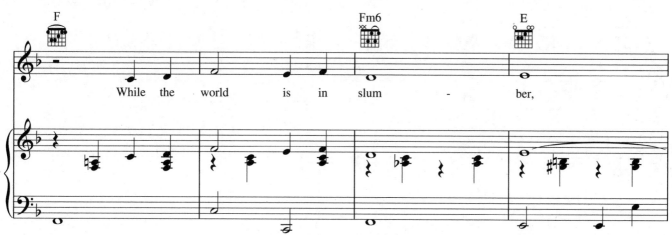

While the world is in slum - ber,

Oh, the times with-out num - ber, Dar - ling, when I

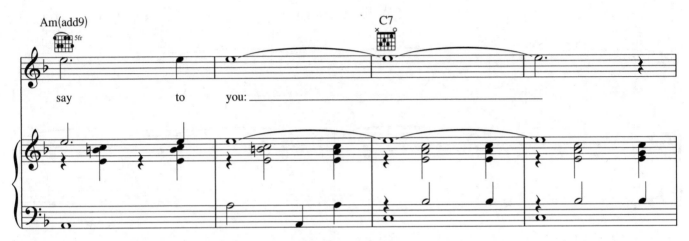

say to you: _____

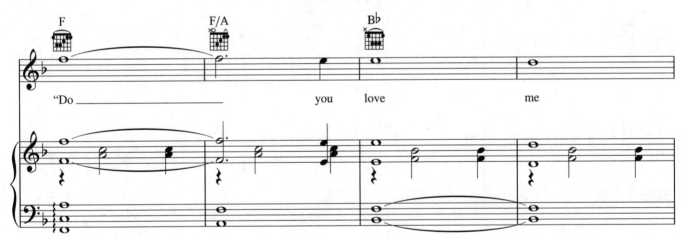

"Do _____ you love me

As I love you? _____

Are you my life - to - be,

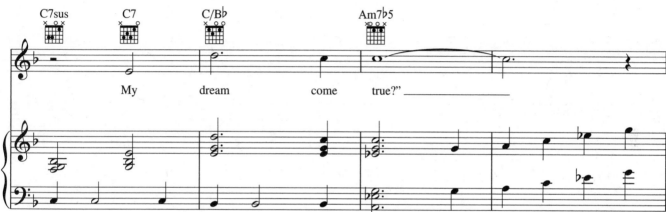

My dream come true?"

Or will this dream of mine

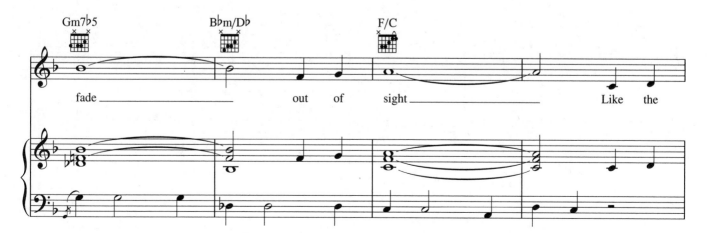

fade out of sight Like the

160

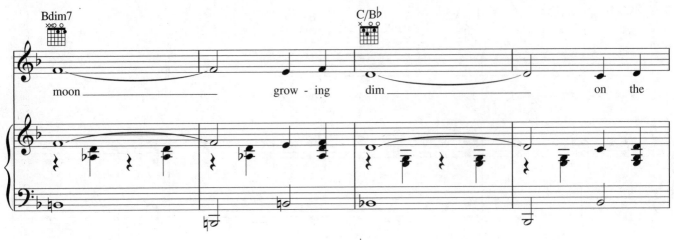

moon _____ grow - ing dim _____ on the

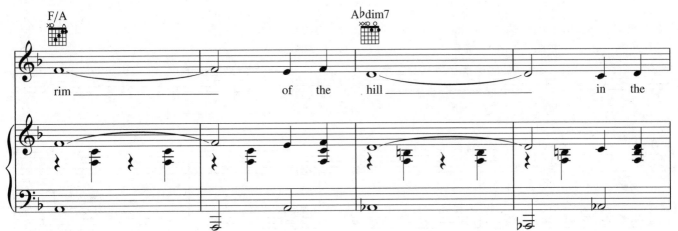

rim _____ of the hill _____ in the

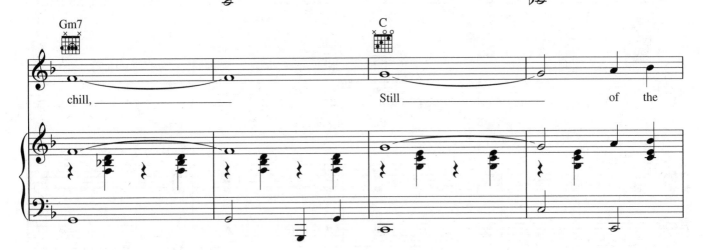

chill, _____ Still _____ of the

night? _____

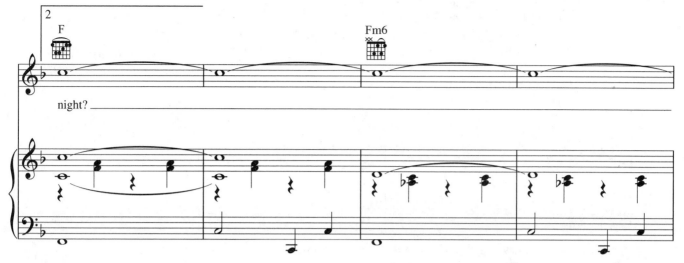

night? _____

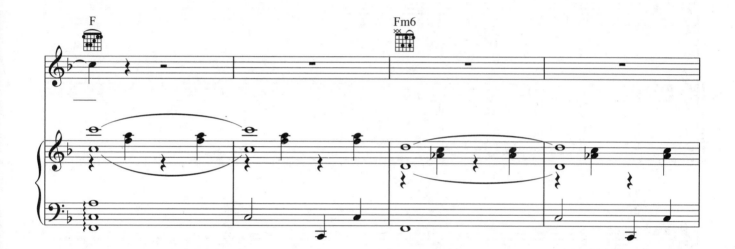

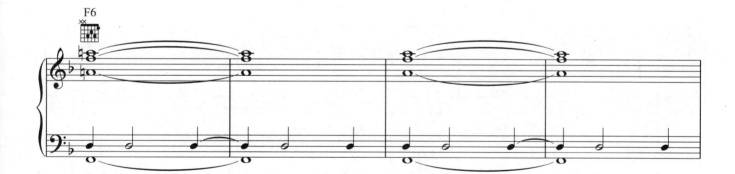

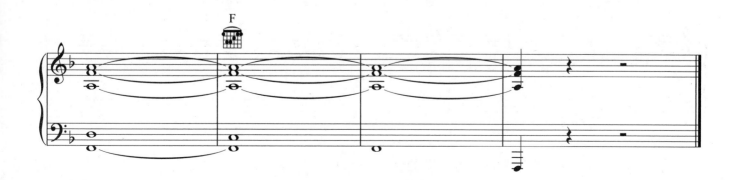

IT COULD HAPPEN TO YOU

from the Paramount Picture AND THE ANGELS SING

Words by JOHNNY BURKE
Music by JAMES VAN HEUSEN

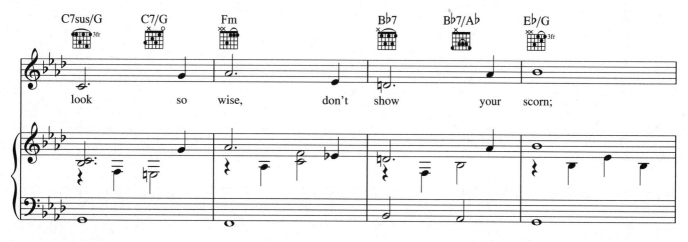

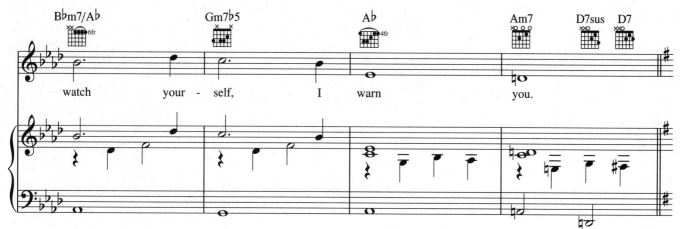

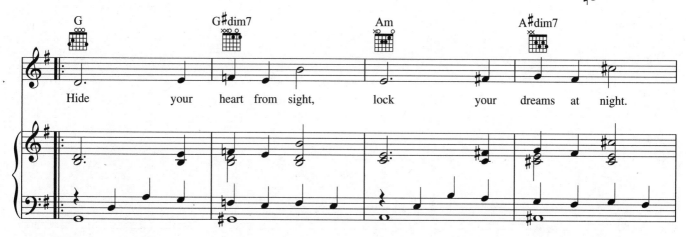

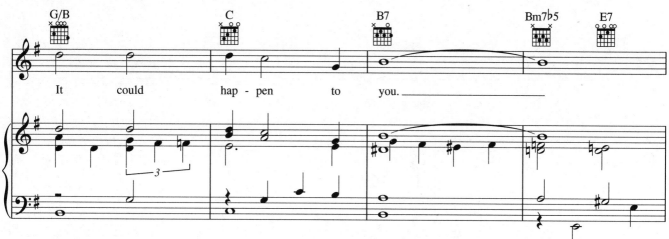

IT'S A MOST UNUSUAL DAY

from A DATE WITH JUDY

Words by HAROLD ADAMSON
Music by JIMMY McHUGH

Moderately, not too slowly

I woke up sing-ing this morn-

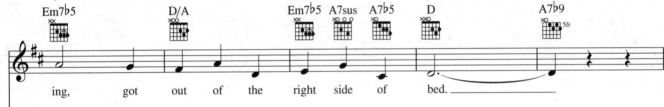

ing, got out of the right side of bed. _____

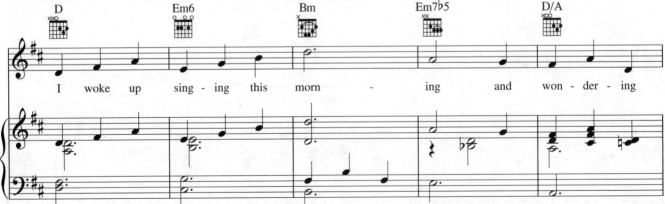

I woke up sing-ing this morn - ing and won-der-ing

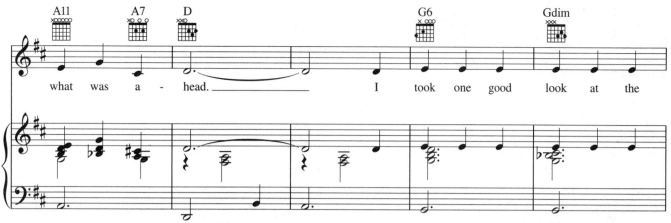

what was a - head. _____ I took one good look at the

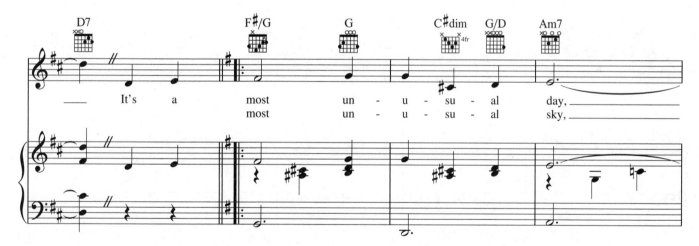

sun _____ and was I the luck - i - est one. _____

It's a most un - u - su - al day, _____

most un - u - su - al sky, _____

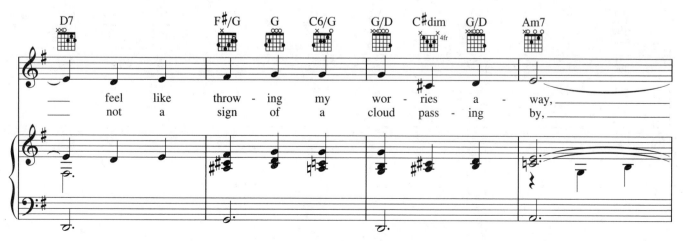

feel like throw - ing my wor - ries a - way, _____

not a sign of a cloud pass - ing by, _____

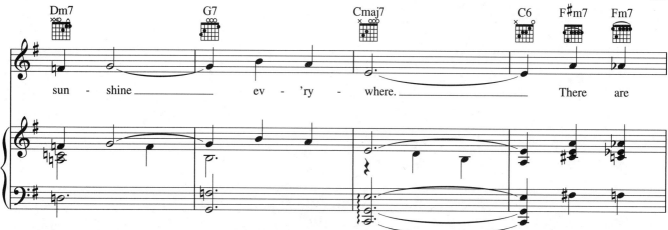

sun - shine _____ ev - 'ry - where. _____ There are

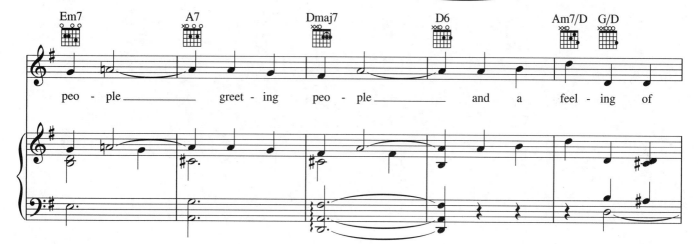

peo - ple _____ greet - ing peo - ple _____ and a feel - ing of

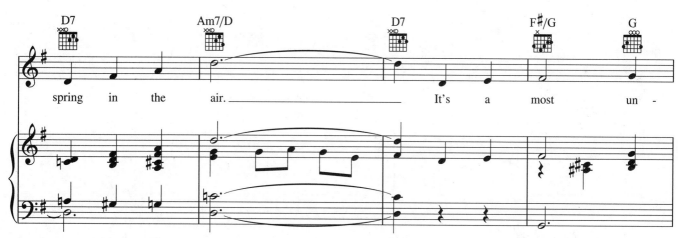

spring in the air. _____ It's a most un -

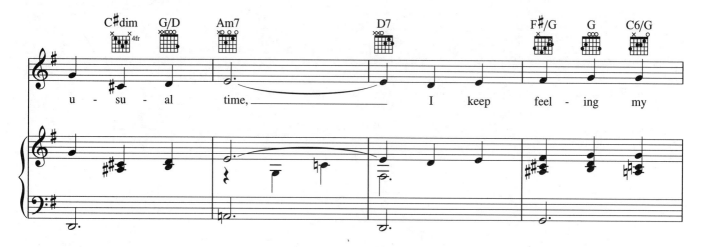

u - su - al time, _____ I keep feel - ing my

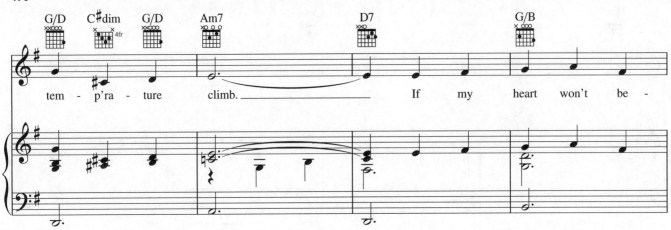

tem - p'ra - ture climb. _____ If my heart won't be -

have in the u - su - al way, well, there's on - ly one thing to

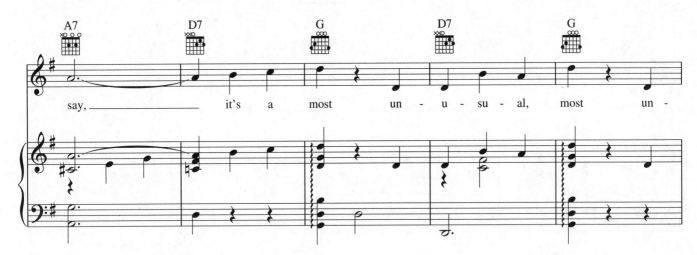

say, _____ it's a most un - u - su - al, most un -

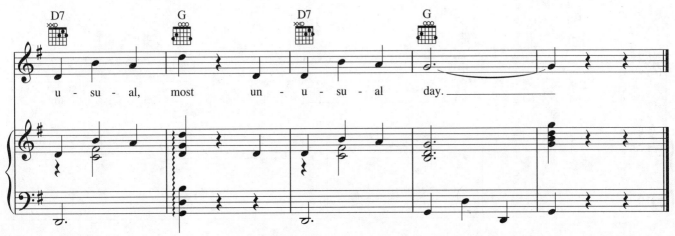

u - su - al, most un - u - su - al day. _____

JUNE IN JANUARY
from the Paramount Picture HERE IS MY HEART

Words and Music by LEO ROBIN
and RALPH RAINGER

just white blos - soms that fall from a - bove, and here is the rea - son, my dear, your mag - ic - al charms.

The night is cold,

the trees are bare, but I can

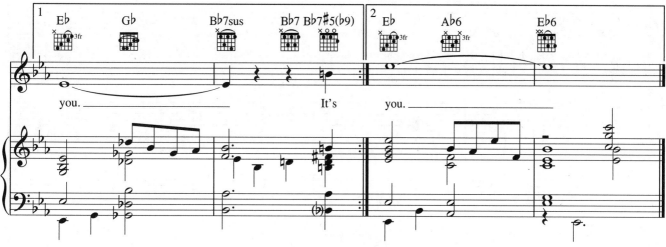

THE LAST TIME I SAW PARIS

from LADY, BE GOOD
from TILL THE CLOUDS ROLL BY

Lyrics by OSCAR HAMMERSTEIN II
Music by JEROME KERN

LONG AGO
(And Far Away)
from COVER GIRL

Words by IRA GERSHWIN
Music by JEROME KERN

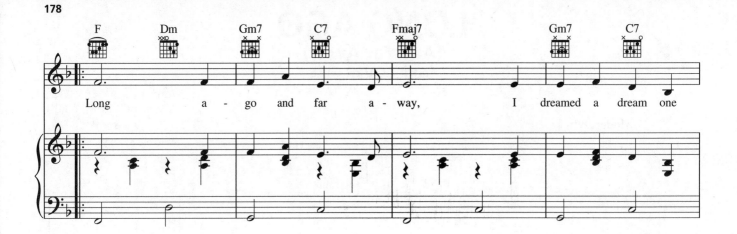

Long a - go and far a - way, I dreamed a dream one

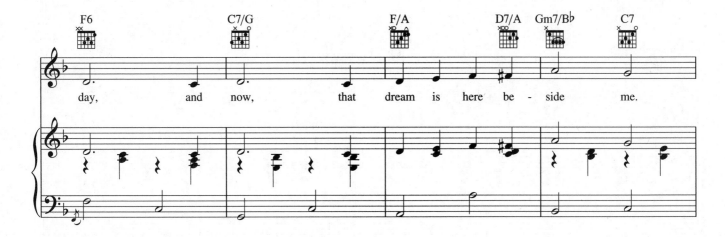

day, and now, that dream is here be - side me.

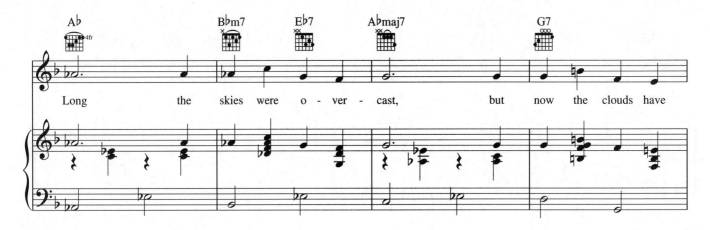

Long the skies were o - ver - cast, but now the clouds have

passed: You're here at last! _____ Chills run

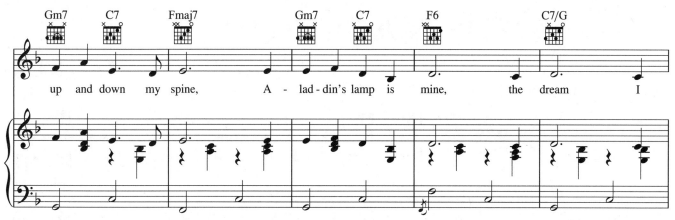

up and down my spine, A - lad - din's lamp is mine, the dream I

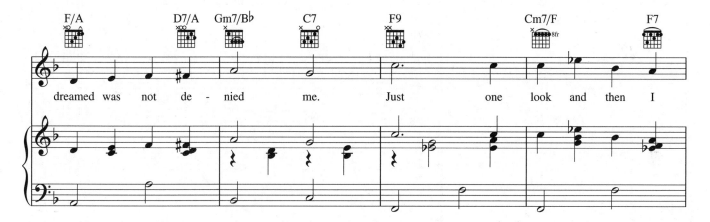

dreamed was not de - nied me. Just one look and then I

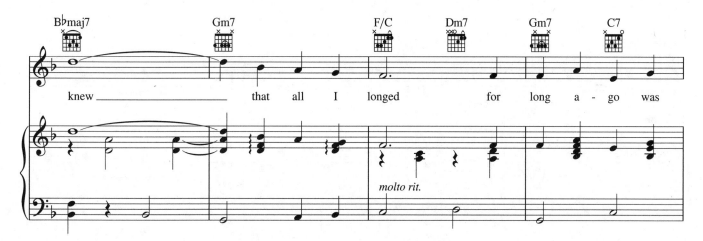

knew _____ that all I longed for long a - go was

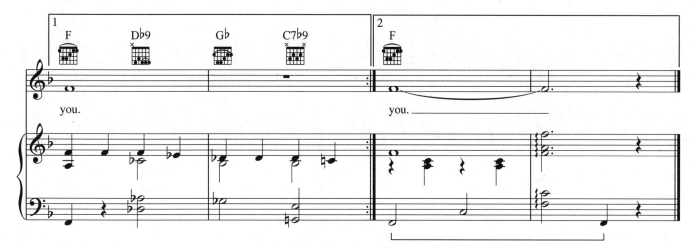

you. you. _____

(You've Got)
THE MAGIC TOUCH

Words and Music by
BUCK RAM

You've got the mag-ic touch. _____ It makes me glow so much. _____ It casts a spell, _____ it rings a bell, the mag-ic touch. _____ Oh, when I

feel your charm, _____ it's like a four - a - larm. _____

__ You make me thrill so much, you've got the mag - ic

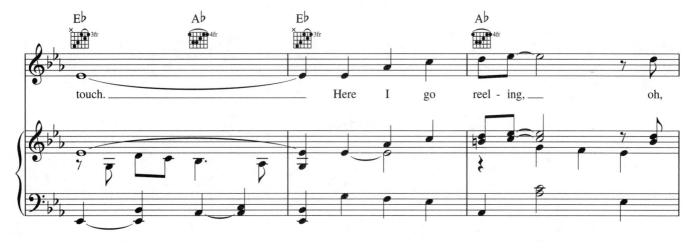

touch. _____ Here I go reel - ing, ___ oh,

oh. I'm feel - ing __ the glow, but where can I

MISTY

Words by JOHNNY BURKE
Music by ERROLL GARNER

Slowly, with expression

185

MAKIN' WHOOPEE!

from WHOOPEE!

Lyrics by GUS KAHN
Music by WALTER DONALDSON

Henry: Ev-'ry time I hear that march from Lo-hen-grin __ I am al-ways on the out-side look-ing in. __ May-be that is why I see the

fun-ny side __ when I see a fall-en broth-er take a bride. __

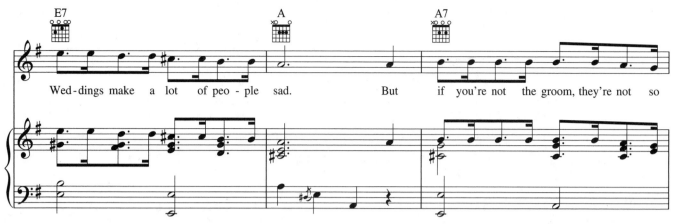

Wed-dings make a lot of peo-ple sad. But if you're not the groom, they're not so

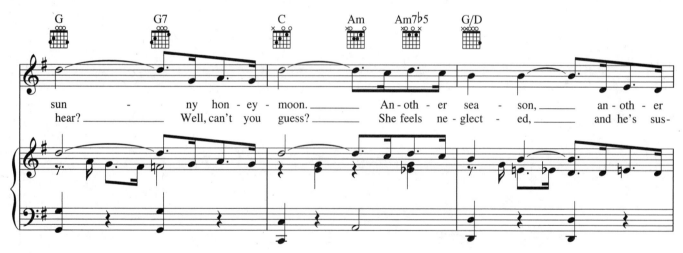

bad. _____ An-oth-er bride, _____ an-oth-er June, _____ an-oth-er
year _____ or may-be less, _____ what's this I

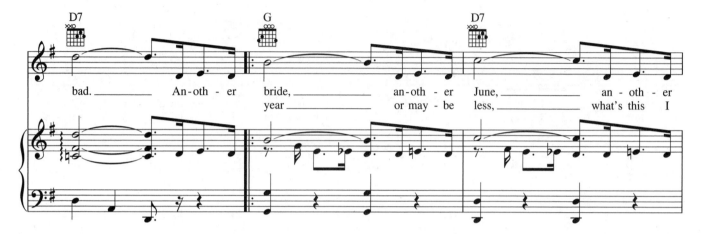

sun - ny hon-ey-moon. _____ An-oth-er sea-son, _____ an-oth-er
hear? _____ Well, can't you guess? _____ She feels ne-glect-ed, _____ and he's sus-

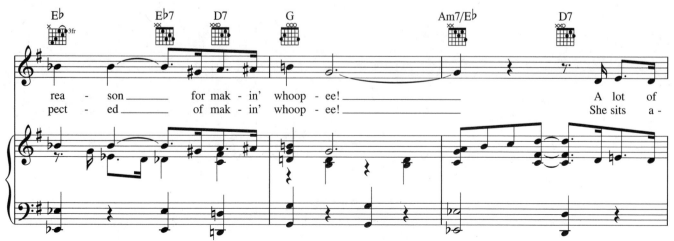

rea-son _____ for mak-in' whoop-ee! _____ A lot of
pect-ed _____ of mak-in' whoop-ee! _____ She sits a-

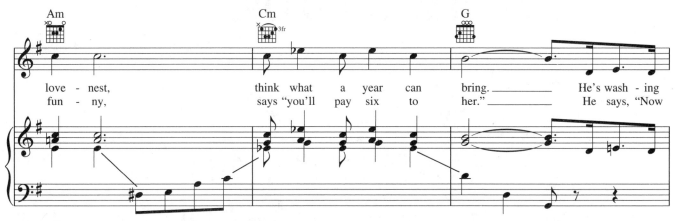

love - nest, think what a year can bring. _____ He's wash - ing
fun - ny, says "you'll pay six to her." _____ He says, "Now

dish - es _____ and ba - by clothes, _____ he's so am - bi - tious, _____ he e - ven
judge, _____ sup - pose I fail?" _____ The judge says, "Budge _____ right in - to

sews. _____ But don't for - get, folks, _____ that's what you get, folks, _____ for mak - in'
jail. _____ You'd bet - ter keep her, _____ I think it's cheap - er _____ than mak - in'

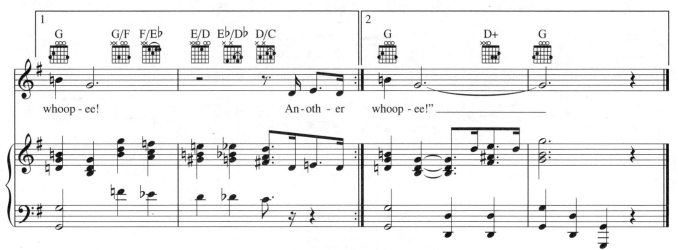

whoop - ee! An - oth - er whoop - ee!" _____

MOONGLOW

Words and Music by WILL HUDSON,
EDDIE DE LANGE and IRVING MILLS

Like some-one that has-n't an-y coun-try, _____ like a stran-ger vis-it-ing from Mars, I went a-round a-lone, just like a roll-ing stone un-til I read a mes-sage in the stars:

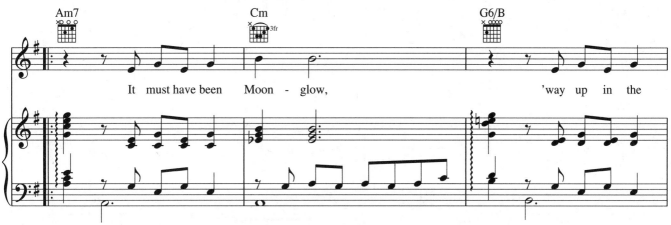

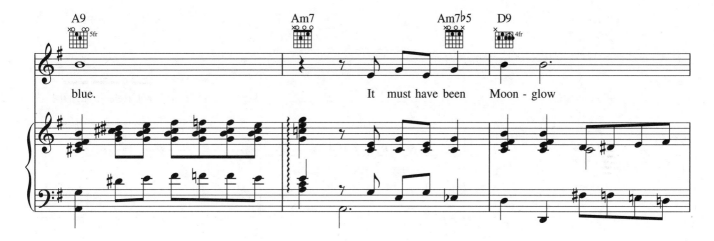

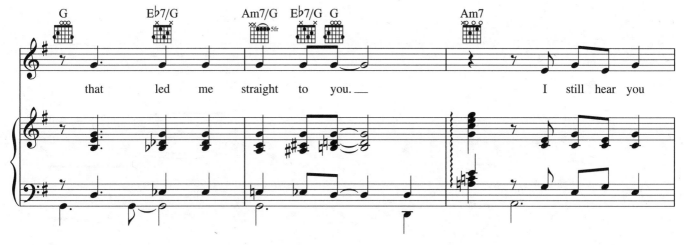

And I start in pray - ing, Oh Lord, please

let this last. __ We _____ seemed to float right through the

air. _____ Heav - en - ly songs _____

__ seemed to come from ev - 'ry - where.

MOONLIGHT BECOMES YOU

from the Paramount Picture ROAD TO MOROCCO

Words by JOHNNY BURKE
Music by JAMES VAN HEUSEN

196

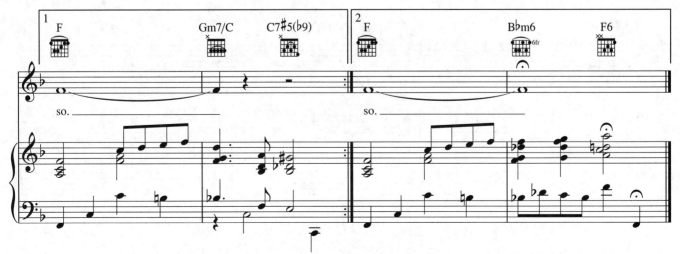

MOONLIGHT IN VERMONT

Words by JOHN BLACKBURN
Music by KARL SUESSDORF

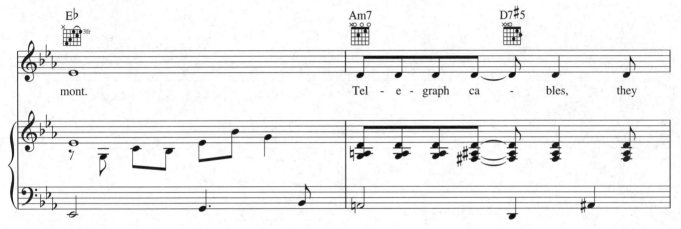

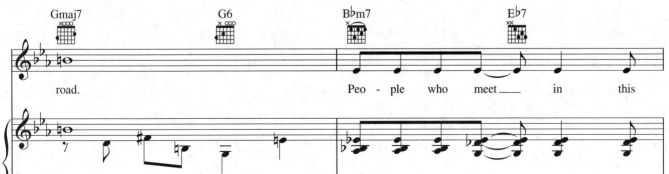

MY BLUE HEAVEN

Lyric by GEORGE WHITING
Music by WALTER DONALDSON

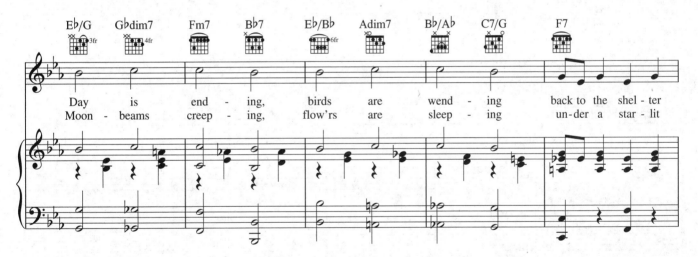

Day is end-ing, birds are wend-ing back to the shel-ter
Moon-beams creep-ing, flow'rs are sleep-ing un-der a star-lit

of each lit-tle nest they love. Night shades fall-ing,
way, wait-ing an-oth-er day. Time for rest-ing,

love birds call - ing. What makes the world go 'round? Noth-ing but love! _____
birds are nest - ing, rest - ing their wea - ry wings, tired _ from play. _____

_____ When whip-poor-wills call _____ and eve-ning is nigh _____ I hur-ry to

my blue heav - en. _____ A turn to the right, _____ a lit-tle white

light _____ will lead you to my blue heav - en. _____ You'll see a

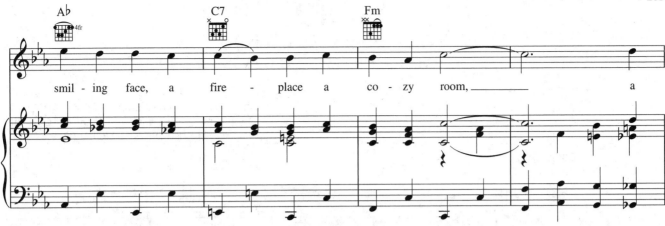

smil - ing face, a fire - place a co - zy room, _____ a

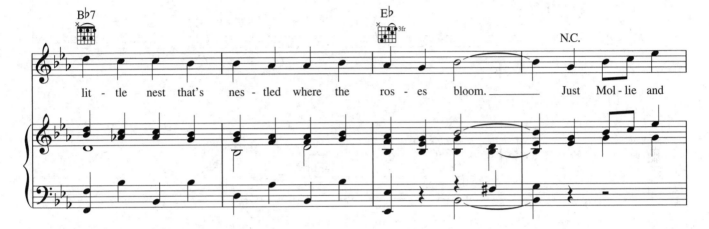

lit - tle nest that's nes - tled where the ros - es bloom. _____ Just Mol - lie and

me _____ and Ba-by makes three. _____ We're hap-py in my

blue _____ heav - en. When whip-poor-wills blue heav - en. _____

MORE
(Ti guarderò nel cuore)
from the Film MONDO CANE

Music by NINO OLIVIERO and RIZ ORTOLANI
Italian Lyrics by MARCELLO CIORCIOLINI
English Lyrics by NORMAN NEWELL

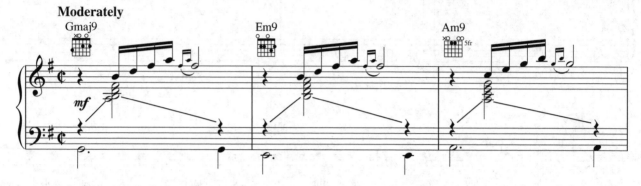

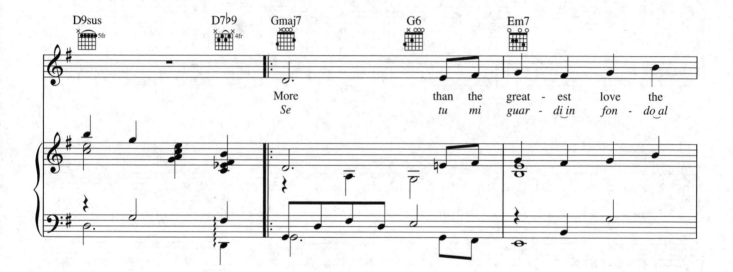

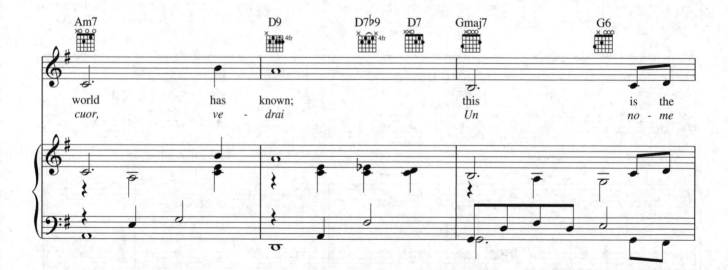

MY FUNNY VALENTINE
from BABES IN ARMS

Words by LORENZ HART
Music by RICHARD RODGERS

made. Thy va - cant brow and thy tous - led hair con -

ceal thy good in - tent. Thou no - ble, up - right,

truth - ful, sin - cere and slight - ly dop - ey gent, you're

my }
My } fun - ny val - en - tine, sweet com - ic

MY IDEAL
from the Paramount Picture PLAYBOY OF PARIS

Words by LEO ROBIN
Music by RICHARD A. WHITING and NEWELL CHASE

MY OLD FLAME

from the Paramount Picture BELLE OF THE NINETIES

Words and Music by ARTHUR JOHNSTON
and SAM COSLOW

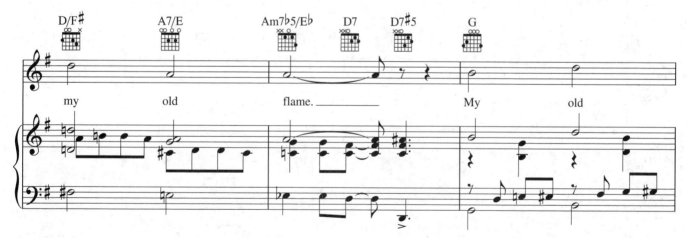

have-n't met a gent so mag-nif-i-cent or el-e-gant___ as my old

flame.___ I've met so man-y who had fas-ci-nat-in' ways,___ a

fas-ci-nat-in' gaze___ in their eyes;___

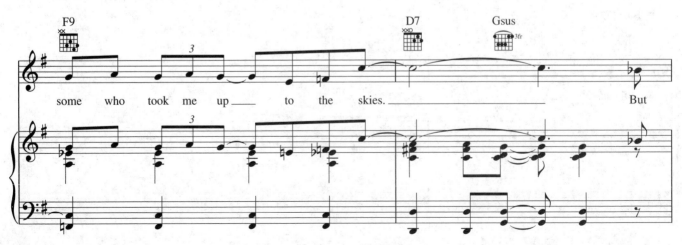

some who took me up___ to the skies.___ But

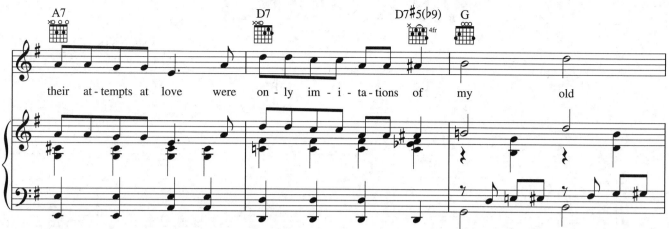

their at-tempts at love were on-ly im-i-ta-tions of my old

flame. _____ I can't e-ven think _ of his name, but I'll

nev-er be the same un-til I dis-cov-er what be-came _ of

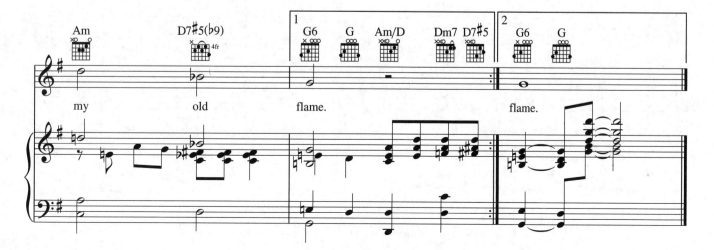

my old flame. flame.

MY ROMANCE

from JUMBO

Words by LORENZ HART
Music by RICHARD RODGERS

MY SILENT LOVE

Words by EDWARD HEYMAN
Music by DANA SUESSE

You would on-ly spurn my love if I had shown it.

You would sure-ly turn my love a-way.

I'm _____ like a flame dy-ing out in the rain, on-ly the ash-es re-main, smoul-d'ring like my si-lent love.

How I long to tell all the things I have planned.

THE NEARNESS OF YOU

from the Paramount Picture ROMANCE IN THE DARK

Words by NED WASHINGTON
Music by HOAGY CARMICHAEL

you're at a dis - tance, but when you are near, oh

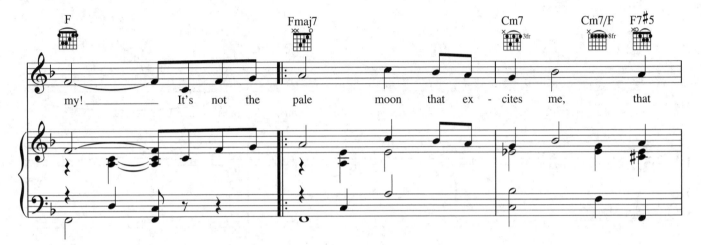

my! _____ It's not the pale moon that ex - cites me, that

thrills and de - lights me. Oh, no,

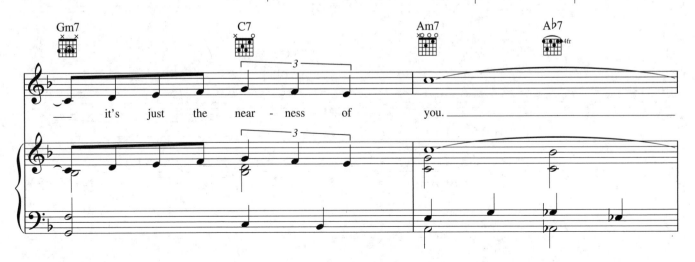

it's just the near - ness of you. _____

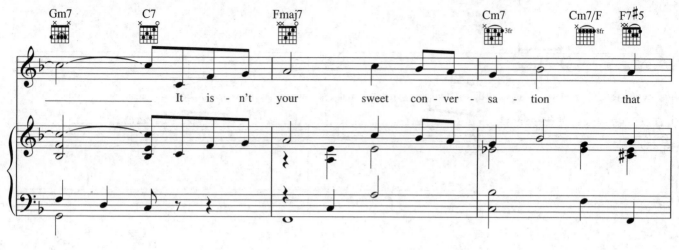

It is - n't your sweet con - ver - sa - tion that

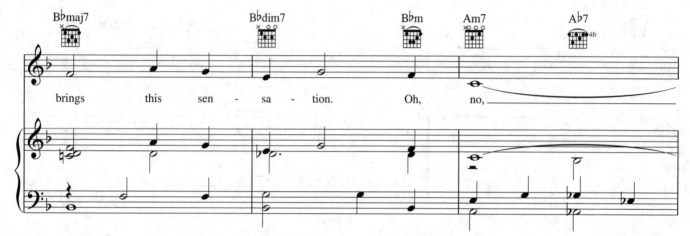

brings this sen - sa - tion. Oh, no, _____

___ it's just the near - ness of you. _____

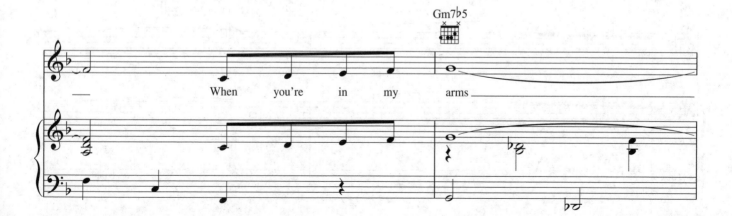

When you're in my arms _____

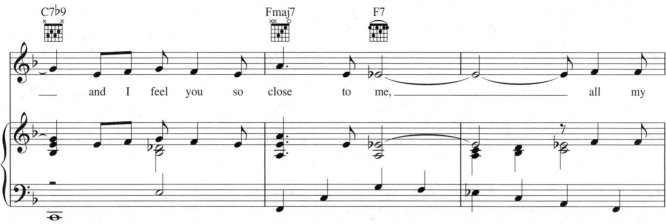

and I feel you so close to me, _____ all my

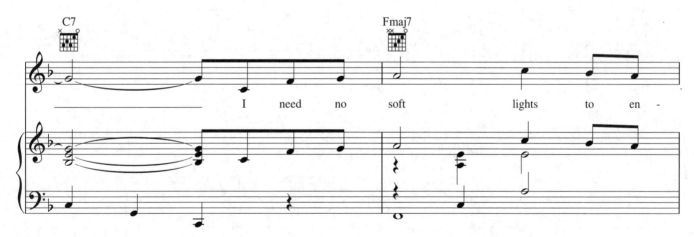

wild - est dreams come true. _____

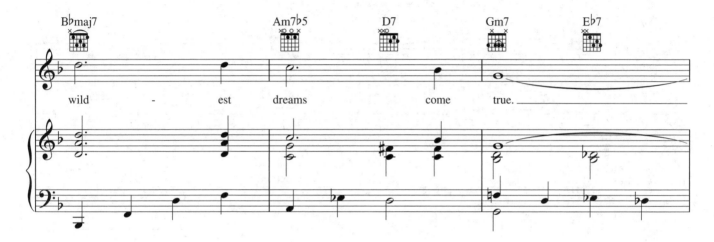

_____ I need no soft lights to en -

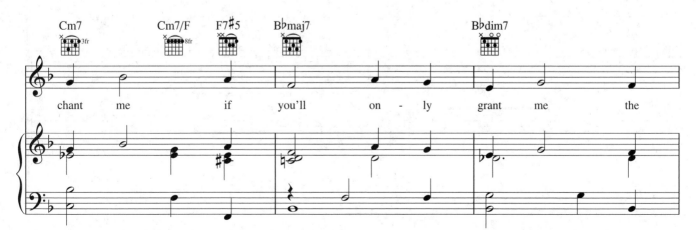

chant me if you'll on - ly grant me the

A NIGHTINGALE SANG IN BERKELEY SQUARE

Lyric by ERIC MASCHWITZ
Music by MANNING SHERWIN

*Pronounced "Bar-kley"

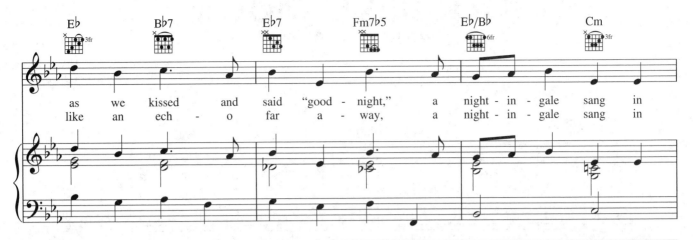

as we kissed and said "good-night," a night-in-gale sang in
like an ech-o far a-way, a night-in-gale sang in

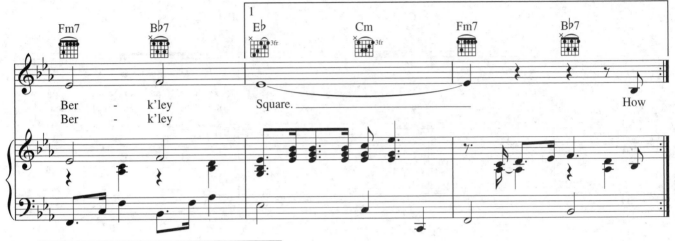

Ber - k'ley Square. _____ How
Ber - k'ley

1
Square.

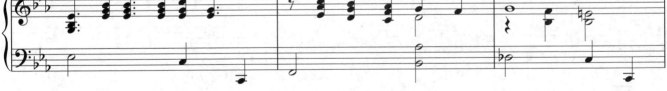

2 Square. I know 'cause I was there

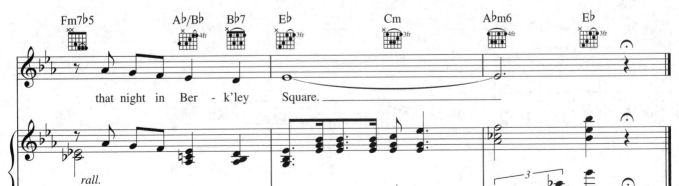

that night in Ber - k'ley Square. _____

rall.

OLD DEVIL MOON
from FINIAN'S RAINBOW

Words by E.Y. HARBURG
Music by BURTON LANE

PENNIES FROM HEAVEN

from PENNIES FROM HEAVEN

Words by JOHN BURKE
Music by ARTHUR JOHNSTON

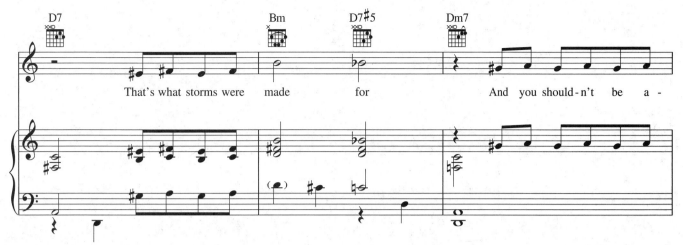

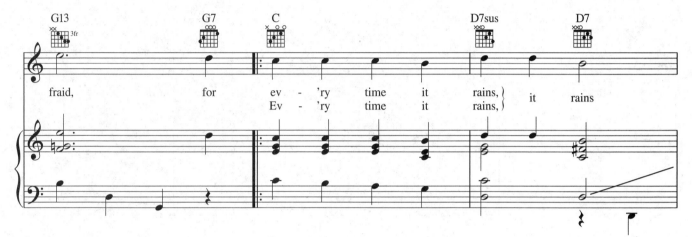

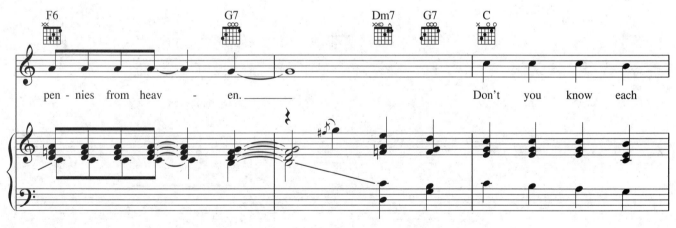

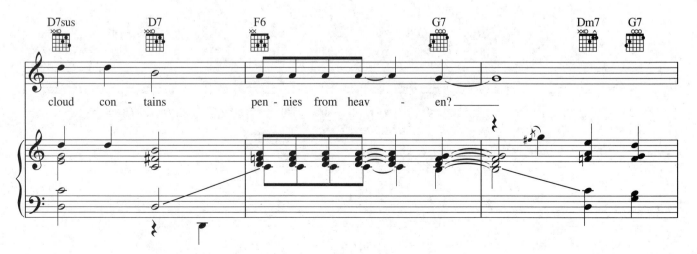

You'll find your for-tune fall-ing all o-ver town.

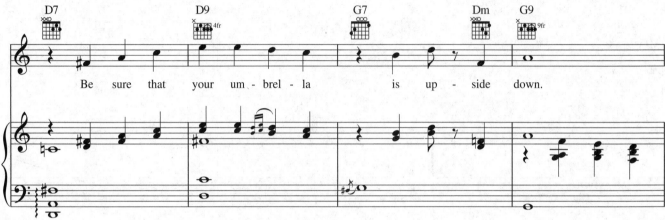

Be sure that your um-brel-la is up-side down.

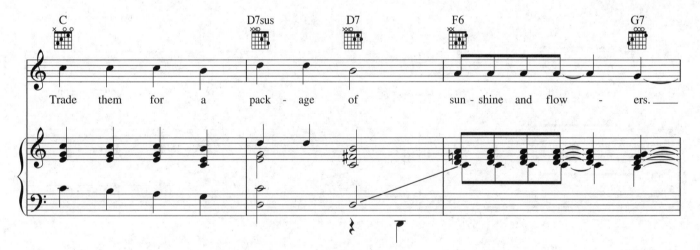

Trade them for a pack-age of sun-shine and flow-ers. ____

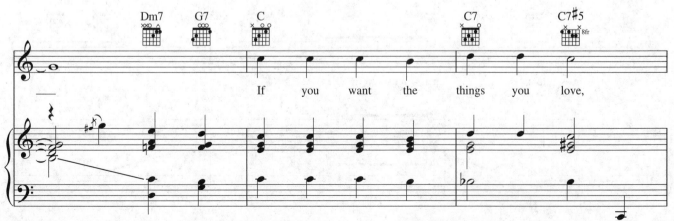

____ If you want the things you love,

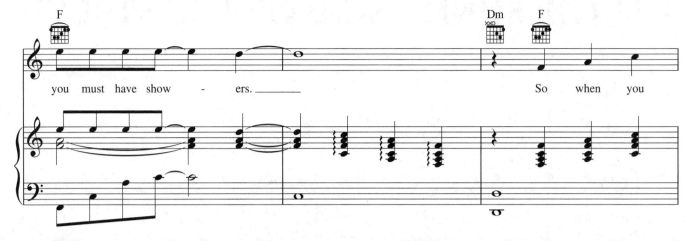

you must have show - ers. _____ So when you

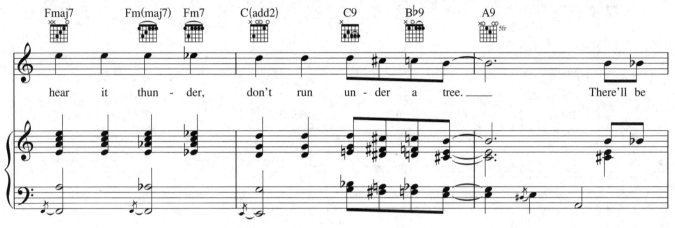

hear it thun - der, don't run un - der a tree. _____ There'll be

pen - nies from heav - en, for you and me. _____

_____ me. _____

ON THE SUNNY SIDE OF THE STREET

Lyric by DOROTHY FIELDS
Music by JIMMY McHUGH

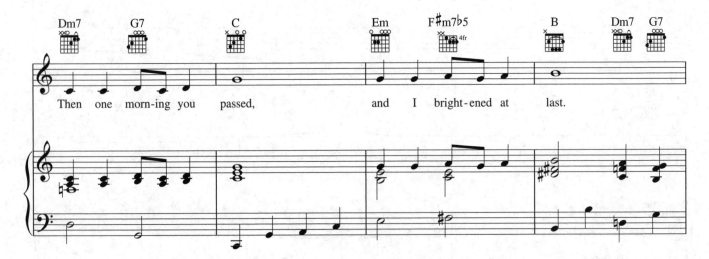

Walked with no one, and talked with no one, and I had noth-ing but shad - ows.

Then one morn-ing you passed, and I bright-ened at last.

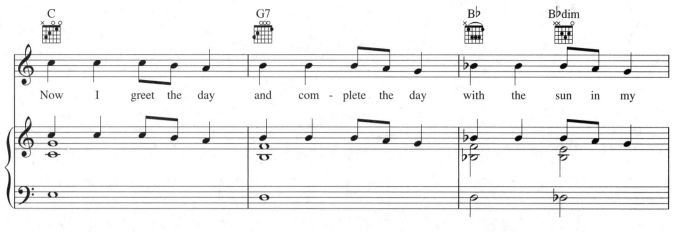

Now I greet the day and com-plete the day with the sun in my

heart. All my wor-ry blew a-way when you taught me how to say: Grab your coat, and get your

hat, leave your wor-ry on the door-step. Just di-rect your

feet to the sun - ny side ___ of the street. Can't you

hear a pit - ter - pat? And that hap - py tune is

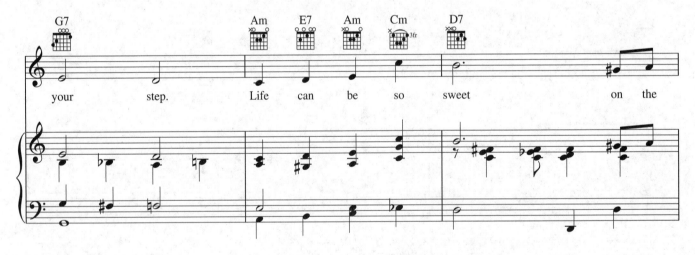

your step. Life can be so sweet on the

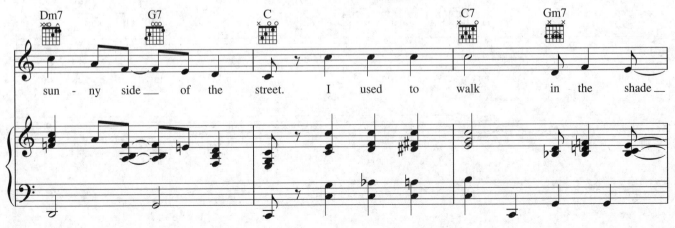

sun - ny side ___ of the street. I used to walk in the shade ___

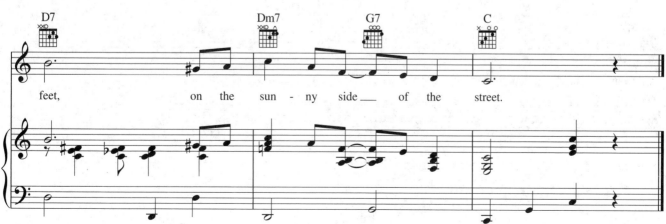

OUT OF NOWHERE

from the Paramount Picture DUDE RANCH

Words by EDWARD HEYMAN
Music by JOHNNY GREEN

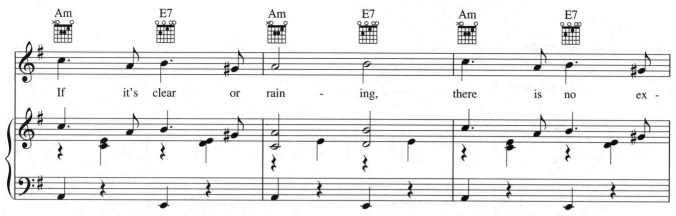

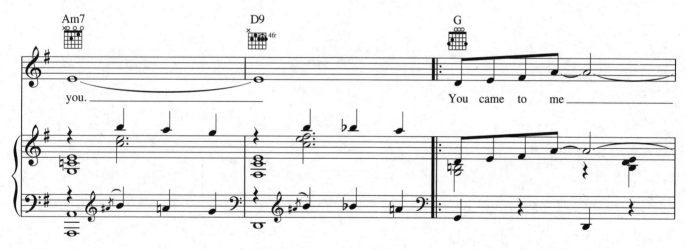

no - where, _____ leav-ing me with _____ a mem-o-

ry, _____ I'll al-ways wait ___ for your re-turn out of

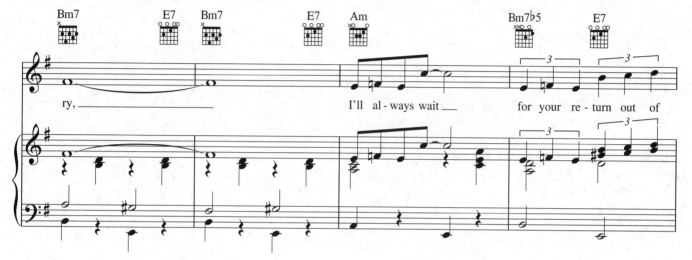

no - where, hop-ing you'll bring your love to

me. me. _____

ROCKIN' CHAIR

Words and Music by
HOAGY CARMICHAEL

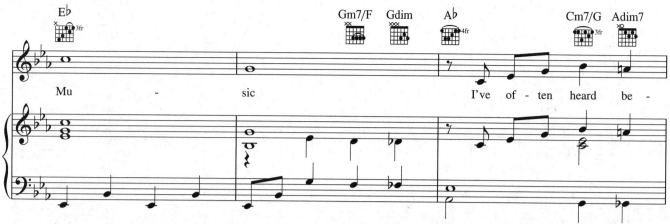

Mu - sic I've of-ten heard be -

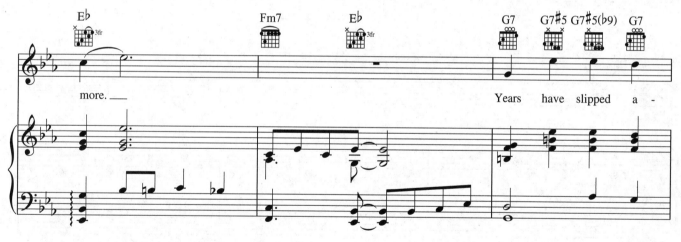

fore, hear't no

more. ___ Years have slipped a -

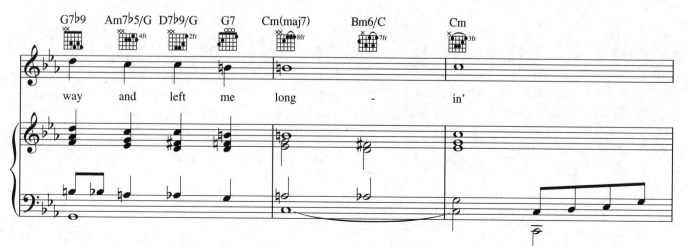

way and left me long - in'

for the days of hap-pi-ness I'll see no

more. Old rock-in' chair's got me, _____

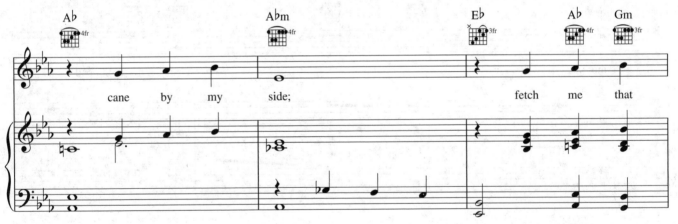

cane by my side; fetch me that

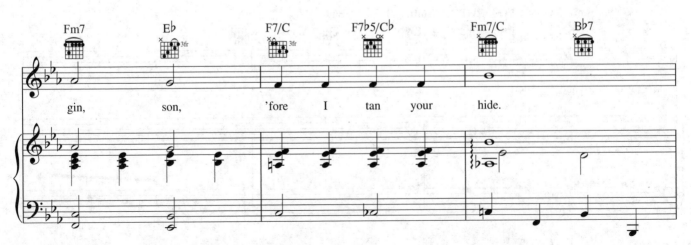

gin, son, 'fore I tan your hide.

SAY IT ISN'T SO

Words and Music by
IRVING BERLIN

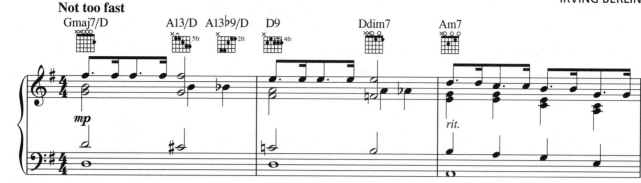

ROUTE 66

By BOBBY TROUP

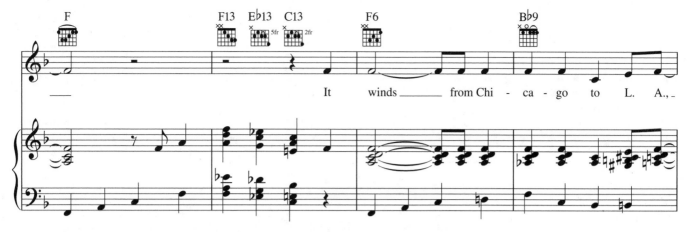

It winds _____ from Chi - ca - go to L. A., _

more than two _____ thou - sand miles all the way. _

Get your kicks on Route _ Six - ty Six! _

Now you go thru Saint Loo - ey, Jop - lin, Mis - sou - ri and

O - kla - ho - ma Cit - y is might - - y pret - ty. You'll see ___ Am - a -

ril - lo, ___ Gal - lup, New Mex - i - co, ___ Flag- staff, Ar - i - zo - na;

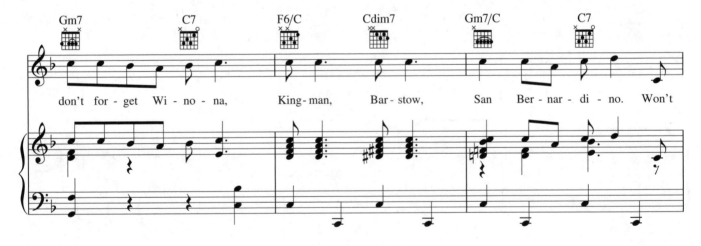

don't for - get Wi - no - na, King - man, Bar - stow, San Ber - nar - di - no. Won't

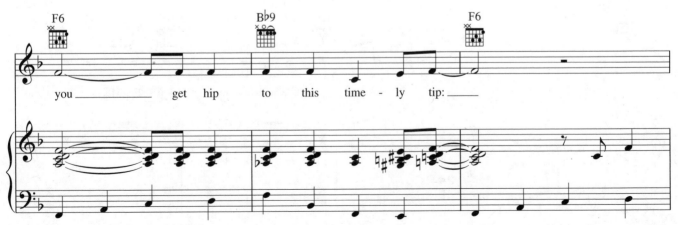

you ___ get hip to this time - ly tip: ___

SENTIMENTAL JOURNEY

Words and Music by BUD GREEN,
LES BROWN and BEN HOMER

heart at ease. _ Gon-na make a sen-ti-men-tal jour-ney to re-new old

mem - o - ries. _ Got my bag, I got my res-er-va-tion, spent each dime I

could af - ford. _ Like a child in wild an - tic - i - pa-tion, long to hear that,

"All ___ a - board." _ Sev - en, _____ that's the time we leave, at

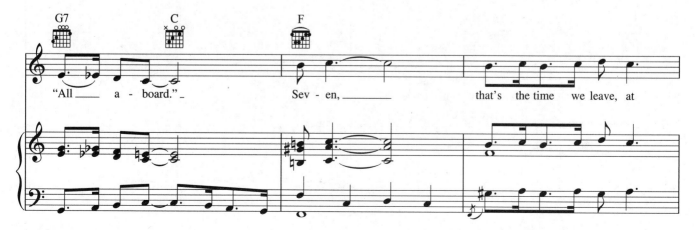

sev - en. _____ I'll be wait - in' up for heav - en, _____

count - in' ev - 'ry mile of rail - road track ___ that takes me back. ___ Nev - er thought my

heart could be so "yearn - y." Why did I de - cide to roam? ___ Got - ta take a

sen - ti - men - tal jour - ney, sen - ti - men - tal jour - ney home. ___ jour - ney home. ___

SENTIMENTAL ME

from the Broadway Musical THE GARRICK GAIETIES

Words by LORENZ HART
Music by RICHARD RODGERS

272

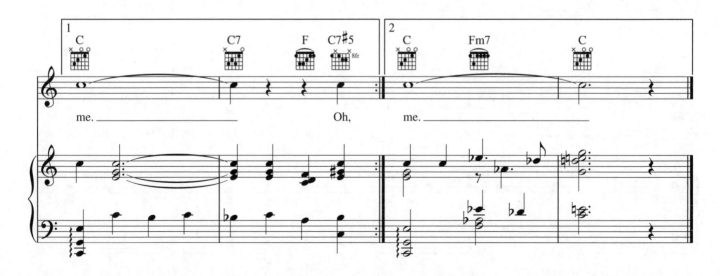

SKYLARK

Words by JOHNNY MERCER
Music by HOAGY CARMICHAEL

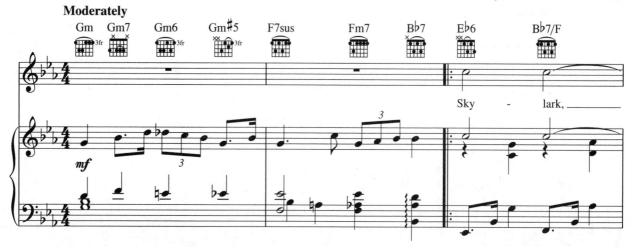

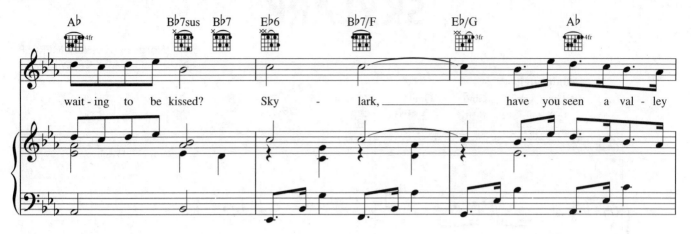

wait - ing to be kissed? Sky - lark, _____ have you seen a val - ley

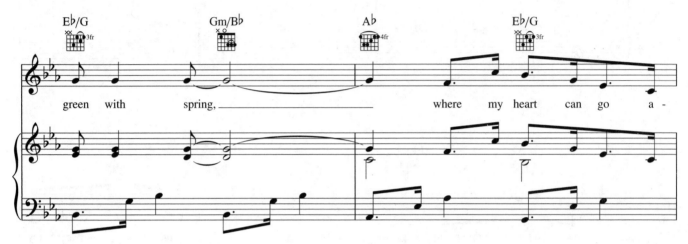

green with spring, _____ where my heart can go a -

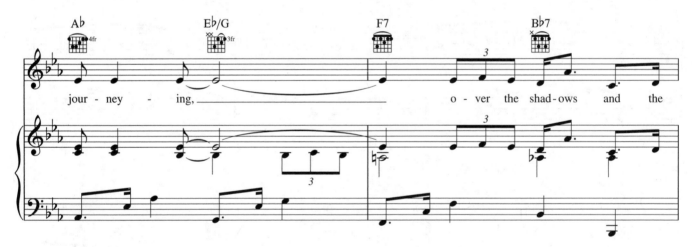

jour - ney - ing, _____ o - ver the shad - ows and the

rain, to a blos - som - cov - ered lane? _____ And in your

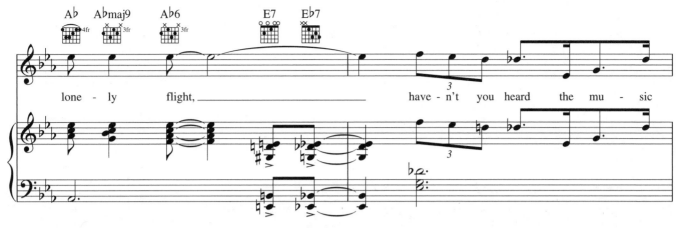

lone - ly flight, _____ have - n't you heard the mu - sic

in the night? _____ Won - der - ful mu - sic,

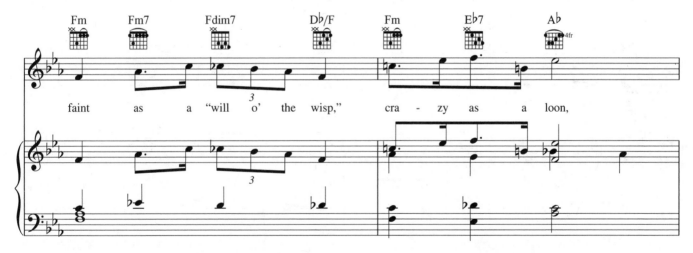

faint as a "will o' the wisp," cra - zy as a loon,

sad as a gyp - sy ser - e - nad - ing the moon. ___ (Oh,)

Sky - lark, _____ I don't know if you can

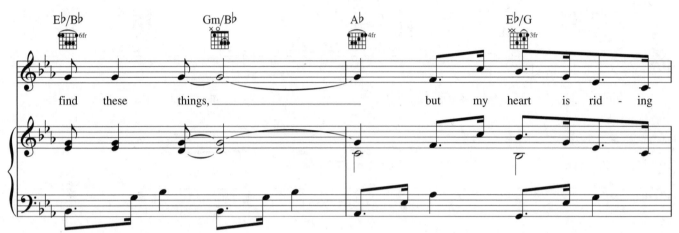

find these things, _____ but my heart is rid - ing

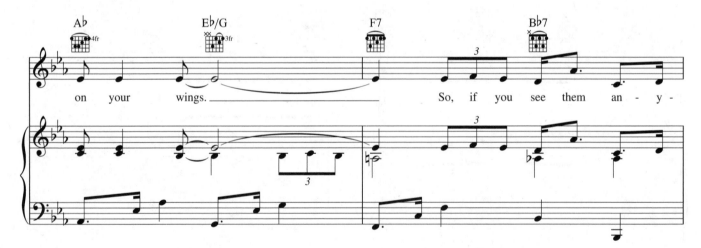

on your wings. _____ So, if you see them an - y -

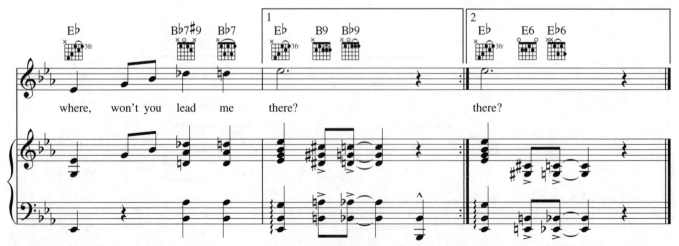

where, won't you lead me there? there?

SMALL FRY

from the Paramount Picture SING, YOU SINNERS

Words by FRANK LOESSER
Music by HOAGY CARMICHAEL

SMOKE GETS IN YOUR EYES

from ROBERTA

Words by OTTO HARBACH
Music by JEROME KERN

They said some-day you'll find all who love are blind.

When your heart's on fire, you must re - al - ize smoke gets in your

eyes. So I chaffed them and I

gay - ly laughed to think they could doubt my love.

SO IN LOVE

from KISS ME, KATE

Words and Music by
COLE PORTER

Strange, dear, _____ but true, dear, _____ when I'm close _____ to you, dear, _____

love   with   you,   my   love, _____ am

STORMY WEATHER
(Keeps Rainin' All the Time)

Lyric by TED KOEHLER
Music by HAROLD ARLEN

Slow lament

Don't know why _____ there's no sun up in the sky, Storm-y Weath-er, _____

Since my man and I ain't to-geth-er, _____ keeps rain-in' all _____ the time. _____

Life is bare, _____ gloom and mis-'ry ev-'ry-where, Storm-y Weath-er, _____

Interlude

STRANGERS IN THE NIGHT
adapted from A MAN COULD GET KILLED

Words by CHARLES SINGLETON and EDDIE SNYDER
Music by BERT KAEMPFERT

A SUNDAY KIND OF LOVE

Words and Music by LOUIS PRIMA,
ANITA NYE, STAN RHODES
and BARBARA BELLE

THEY DIDN'T BELIEVE ME

from THE GIRL FROM UTAH

Words by HERBERT REYNOLDS
Music by JEROME KERN

Eb7

smile _____ makes the liv - ing worth the while. _____
"yes," _____ hes - i - tat - ing more or less. _____

Fm

Fm/Ab

___ So I've got to run a - round _____ tell - ing peo - ple what I've
___ And you kissed me where I stood _____ just like an - y fel - low

Cm/G   **G7**

Cm   **G**   **Eb7**   **Eb7**

found. _____ And when I told them _____
would. _____ And when I told them _____

N.C.

Ab

___ how beau - ti - ful you are, _____ they did - n't be -
___ how won - der - ful you are, _____ they did - n't be -

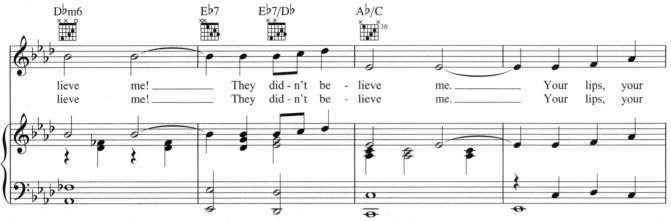

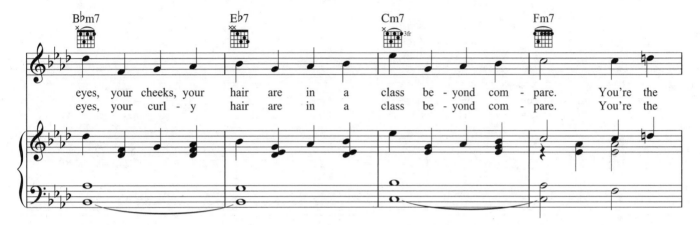

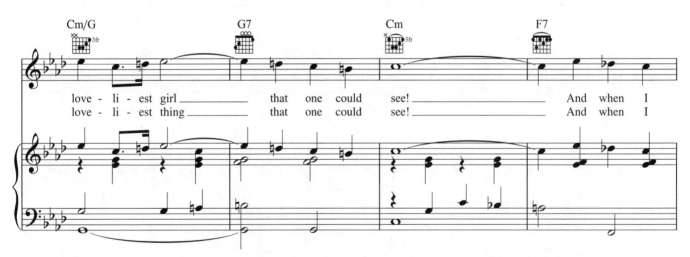

that I'm the man whose wife one day you'll be, ____
that I'm the girl whose boy one day you'll be, ____

__ they'll nev-er be-lieve me. ____ They'll nev-er be-
__ they'll nev-er be-lieve me. ____ They'll nev-er be-

lieve me ____ that from this great big world you've cho - sen
lieve me ____ that from this great big world you've cho - sen

me! ____ And when I   me! ____

THIS CAN'T BE LOVE
from THE BOYS FROM SYRACUSE

Words by LORENZ HART
Music by RICHARD RODGERS

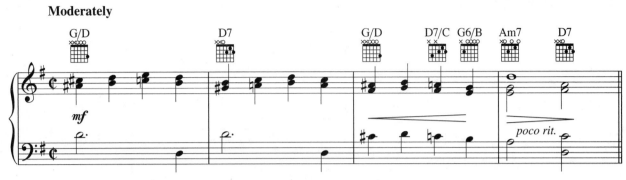

In Ve- ro- na my late cous- in Ro- me- o _____

Was three times as stu- pid as my Dro- mi- o. _____

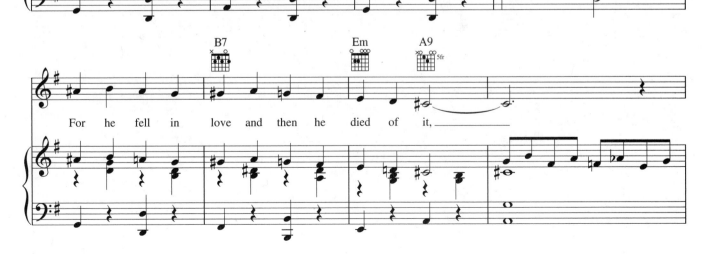

For he fell in love and then he died of it, _____

Smoothly

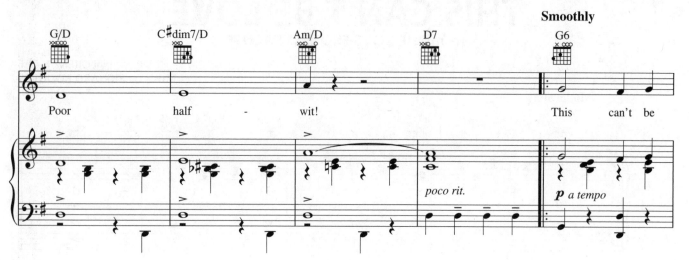

Poor half - wit! This can't be

love be - cause I feel so well, _____ No sobs, no sor -

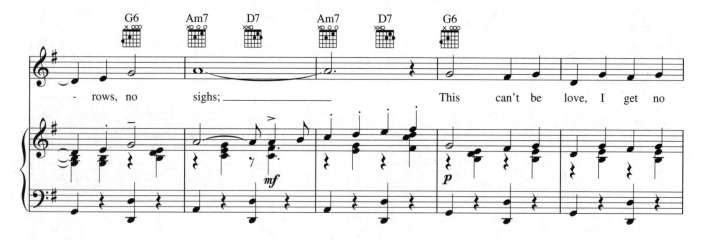

- rows, no sighs; _____ This can't be love, I get no

diz - zy spell. _____ My head is not _____ in the

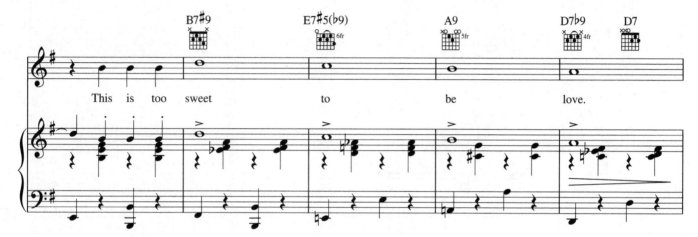

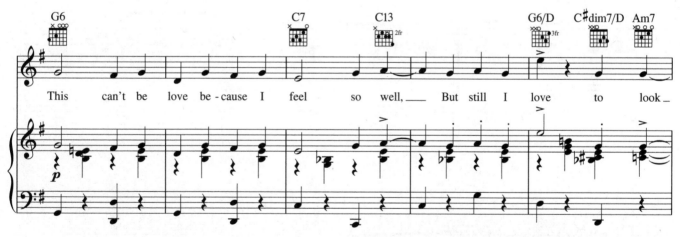

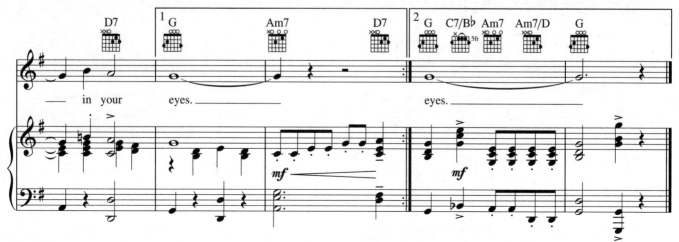

THE THINGS WE DID LAST SUMMER

Words by SAMMY CAHN
Music by JULE STYNE

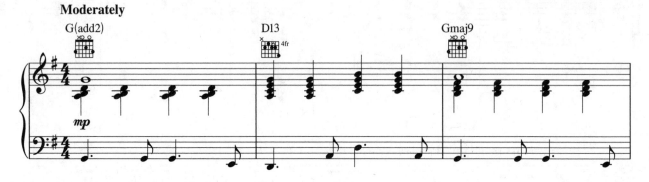

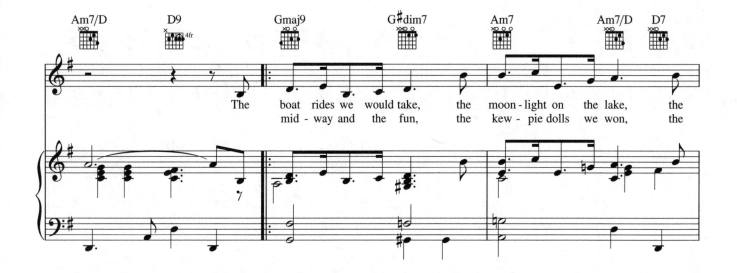

The boat rides we would take, the moon-light on the lake, the
mid-way and the fun, the kew-pie dolls we won, the

way we danced and hummed our fav-'rite song. The
bell {I / you} rang to prove that {I was / you were} strong. The

The leaves be-gan to fade like prom-is-es we made. How

could a love that seemed so right go wrong? The things we did last

sum-mer I'll re-mem-ber _____ all win-ter long.

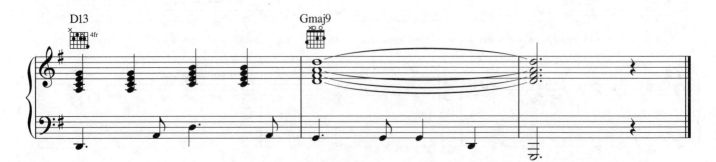

TOO LATE NOW

from ROYAL WEDDING

Words by ALAN JAY LERNER
Music by BURTON LANE

Too late now to for-get your smile; the way we cling when we've danced a-while; too late now to for-get and go on to some-one new.

Too late now to for-get your voice; the way one word makes my

heart re - joice; too late now to i - mag - ine my - self a -

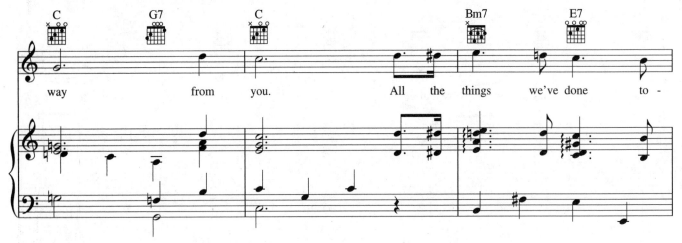

way from you. All the things we've done to -

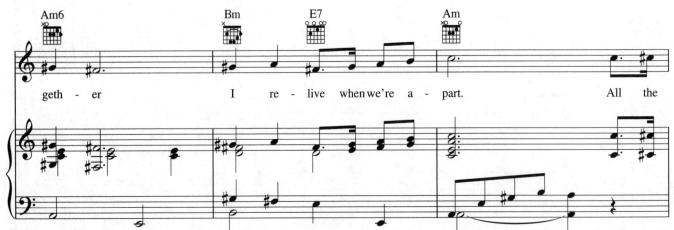

geth - er I re - live when we're a - part. All the

ten - der fun to - geth - er stays on in my heart.

How could I ev - er close the door, and be the same as I was be - fore?

Dar - ling, no, no, I can't an - y - more; it's too late

1

now. _____

2

now. _____

THE WAY YOU LOOK TONIGHT

from SWING TIME

Words by DOROTHY FIELDS
Music by JEROME KERN

Some - day when I'm aw-f'ly low, when the world is
love - ly, with your smile so warm, and your cheek so

cold, I will feel a glow just think-ing of you
soft, there is noth-ing for me but to love you,

and the way you look to - night. _____
just the way you look to - night. _____ Oh, but you're

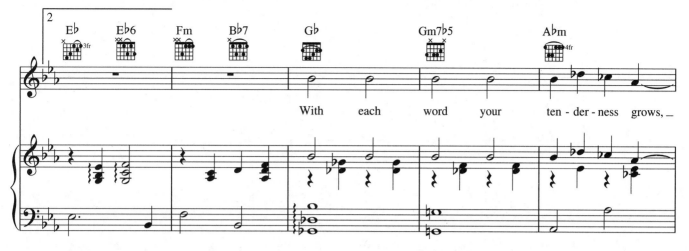

With each word your ten - der - ness grows, __

__ tear - ing my fear __ a - part, _____

and that laugh that wrin - kles your nose ____ touch - es my

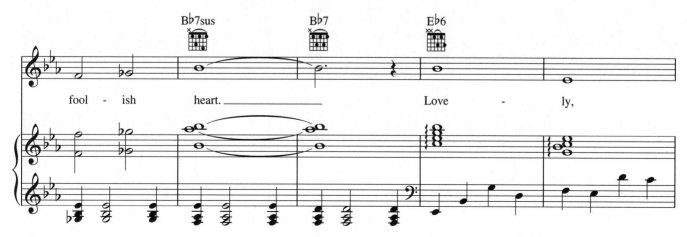

fool - ish heart. _____ Love - ly,

never, nev-er change, keep that breath-less charm,

won't you please ar-range it, 'cause I love you,

rall.

just the way you look to-night.

a tempo

Just the way you look to-night. _____

rall.

TWO SLEEPY PEOPLE

from the Paramount Motion Picture THANKS FOR THE MEMORY

Words by FRANK LOESSER
Music by HOAGY CARMICHAEL

Tick, tock! Cuck - oo! Here we are, out of cig - a - rettes, __
Here we are, in the co - zy chair, __

hold - ing hands and yawn - ing, look how late it gets. __
pick - ing on a wish - bone from the Frig - i - daire. __

Two sleep - y peo - ple by dawn's ear - ly light, and
Two sleep - y peo - ple with noth - ing to say, and

too much in love to say "Good - night."

THE VERY THOUGHT OF YOU

Words and Music by
RAY NOBLE

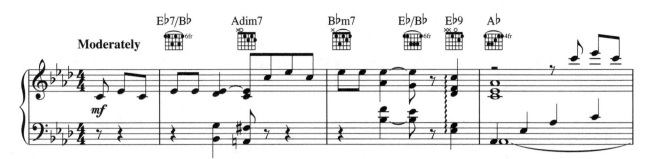

I don't need your pho - to - graph _____
I hold you re - spon - si - ble, _____

_____ to keep _____ by my bed;
_____ I'll take _____ it to law,

Your pic - ture is
I nev - er have

al - ways in _____ my head. _____
felt like this _____ be - fore. _____

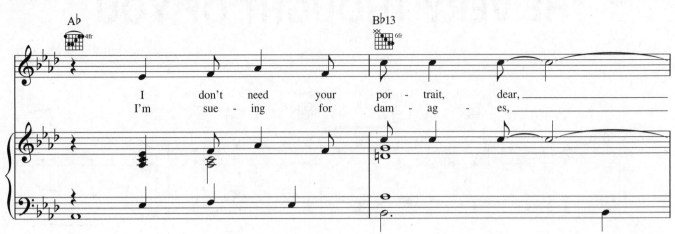

Ab   Bb13

I don't need your por-trait, dear, _____
I'm sue-ing for dam-ag - es, _____

Eb7   Edim7   Fm   Fm7   Fm7b5

_ to call _ you to mind, _____ for sleep-ing or
_ ex-cus - es won't do, _____ I'll on - ly be

Abmaj7/Bb   Bb13b9   Bbm7

wak - ing, dear, _____ I find: _____
sat - is - fied _____ with you. _____

With a slow, easy swing (♪♪ = ♪ ♪)

Eb9   N.C.   Ab

The ver - y thought of you, _____ and I for-

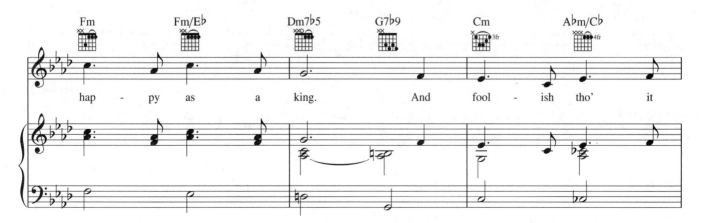

WHAT A DIFF'RENCE A DAY MADE

English Words by STANLEY ADAMS
Music and Spanish Words by MARIA GREVER

WHEN I FALL IN LOVE

from ONE MINUTE TO ZERO

Words by EDWARD HEYMAN
Music by VICTOR YOUNG

WITCHCRAFT

Music by CY COLEMAN
Lyrics by CAROLYN LEIGH

Medium bounce

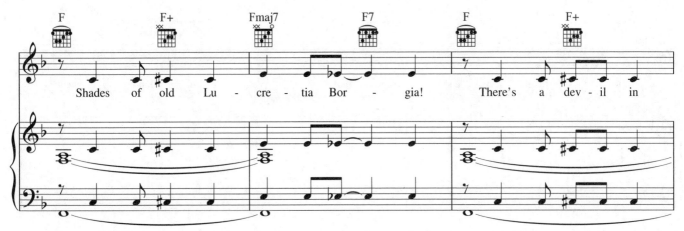

Shades of old Lu-cre-tia Bor-gia! There's a dev-il in

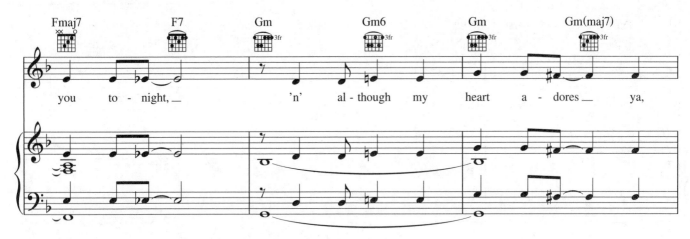

you to-night, __ 'n' al-though my heart a-dores __ ya,

my head says __ it ain't right, __ right to let you

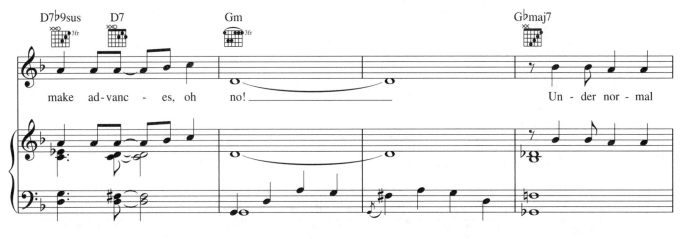

make ad-vanc - es, oh no! _____ Un - der nor - mal

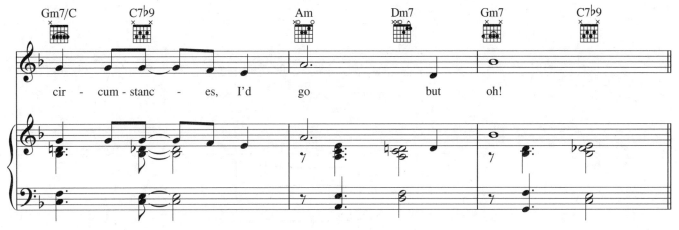

cir - cum - stanc - es, I'd go but oh!

Those fin - gers in my hair, ___ that sly, come -

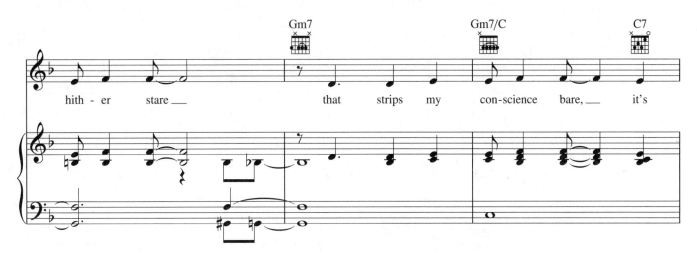

hith - er stare ___ that strips my con-science bare, ___ it's

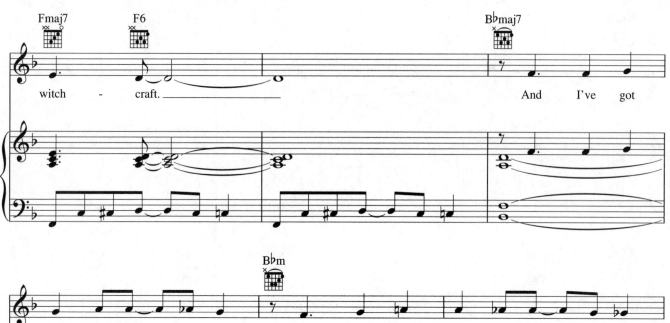

witch - craft. _____ And I've got

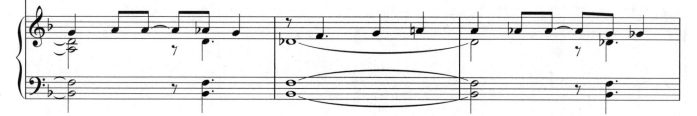

no de - fense ___ for it, the heat is too in - tense ___ for it,

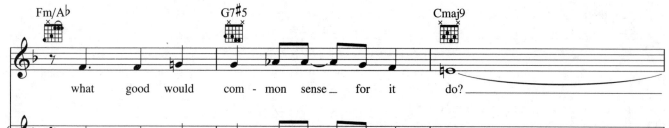

what good would com - mon sense ___ for it do? _____

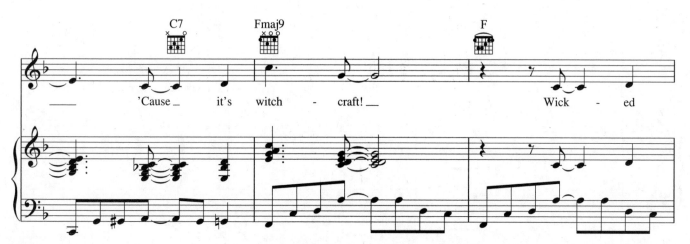

___ 'Cause ___ it's witch - craft! ___ Wick - ed

witch - craft. _ And _ al - though I _ know _

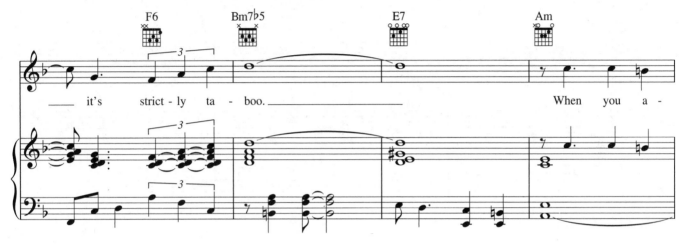

_ it's strict - ly ta - boo. _ When you a -

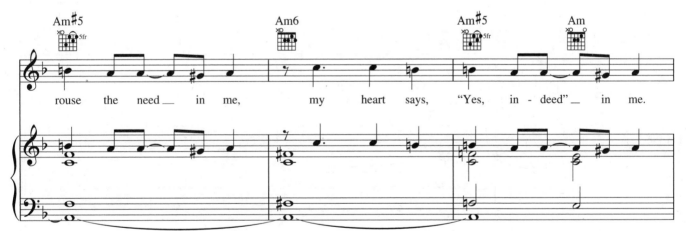

rouse the need _ in me, my heart says, "Yes, in - deed" _ in me.

"Pro - ceed with what you're lead - in' me to!" _

It's such an an-cient pitch ___ but one I would-n't switch ___ 'cause there's no

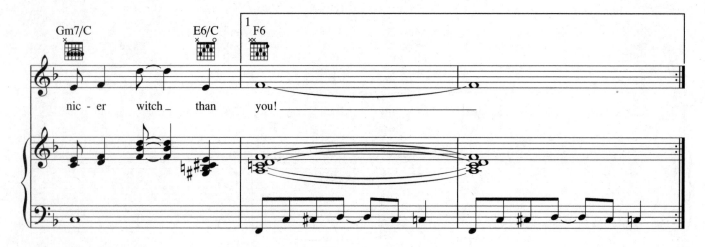

nic-er witch ___ than you! _____

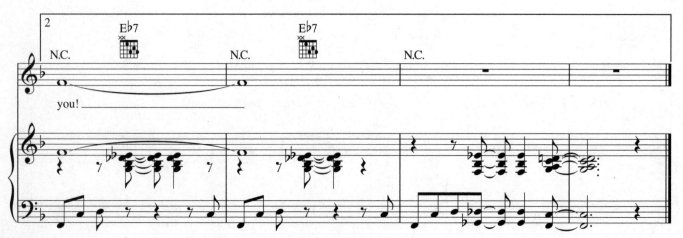

you! _____

WHERE OR WHEN
from BABES IN ARMS

Words by LORENZ HART
Music by RICHARD RODGERS

Things you do _____ come back to you, _____ as though they knew the way. Oh, the

tricks your mind can play! It seems we stood and talked like

this be - fore. We looked at each oth - er in the same way then,

but I can't re - mem - ber where or when. _____

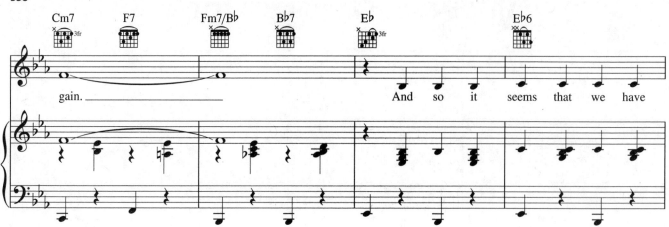

And so it seems that we have

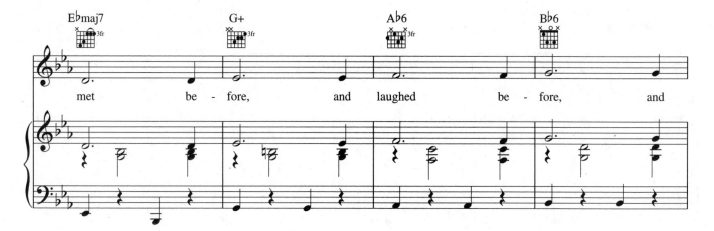

met be - fore, and laughed be - fore, and

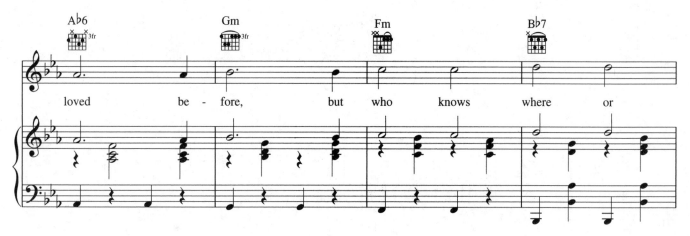

loved be - fore, but who knows where or

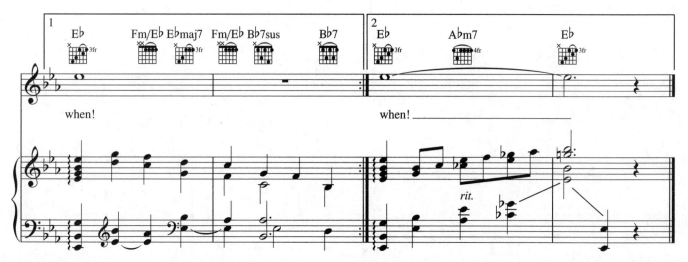

when! when!

WIVES AND LOVERS
(Hey, Little Girl)
from the Paramount Picture WIVES AND LOVERS

Words by HAL DAVID
Music by BURT BACHARACH

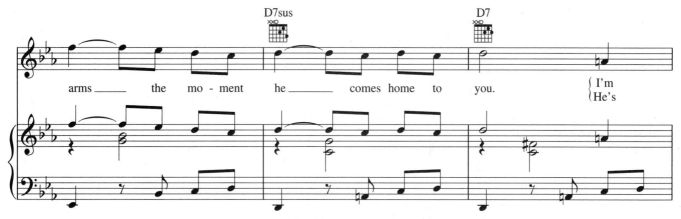

arms _____ the mo - ment he _____ comes home to you. { I'm
{ He's

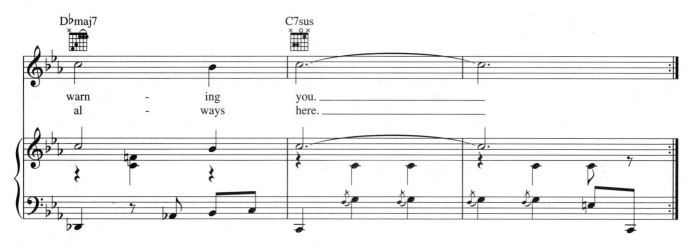

warn - ing you. _____
al - ways here. _____

Hey, lit - tle girl, bet - ter wear some - thing pret - ty,

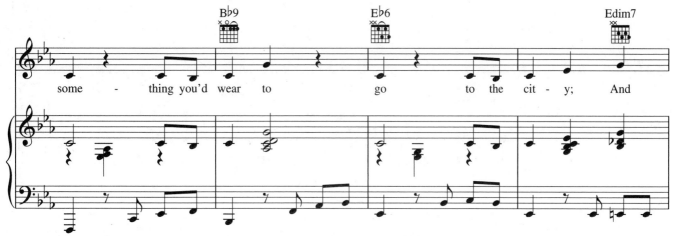

some - thing you'd wear to go to the cit - y; And

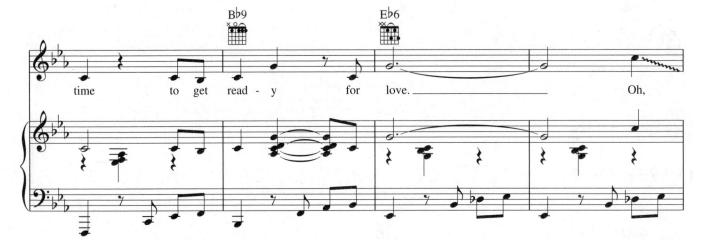

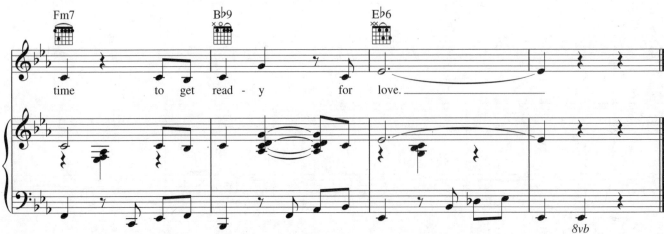

8vb

YESTERDAY ONCE MORE

Words and Music by JOHN BETTIS
and RICHARD CARPENTER

Moderate Ballad

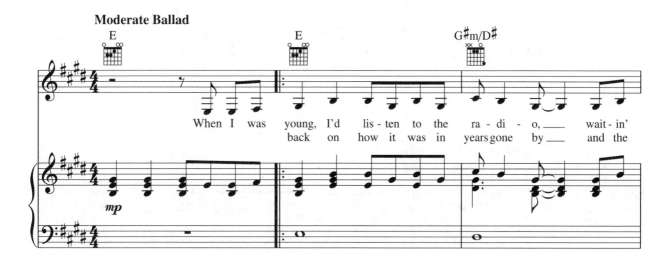

When I was young, I'd lis-ten to the ra-di-o, ___ wait-in'
back on how it was in years gone by ___ and the

for my fa-v'rite songs. ___ When they played, I'd sing a-long; ___
good times that I had, ___ makes to-day seem rath-er sad; ___

___ it made me smile. ___ Those were such
___ so much has changed. ___ It was

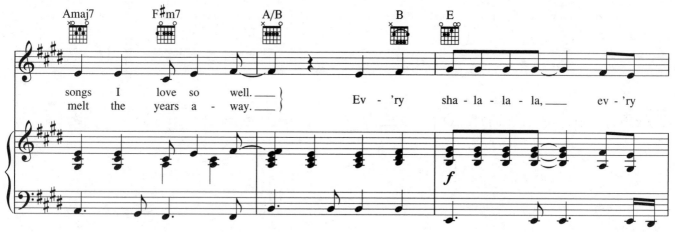

shing - a - ling - a - ling that they're start - ing to sing's_ so fine. ___

When they get to the part ___ where he's break - in' her heart, _ it can
All my best mem - o - ries ___ come back clear - ly to me; ___ some can

real - ly make me cry ___ } just like be - fore. ___
e - ven make me cry ___ }

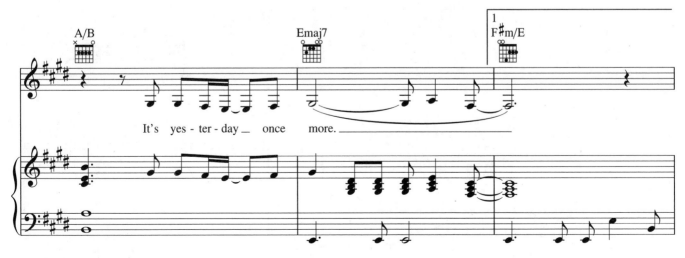

It's yes - ter - day ___ once more. _____

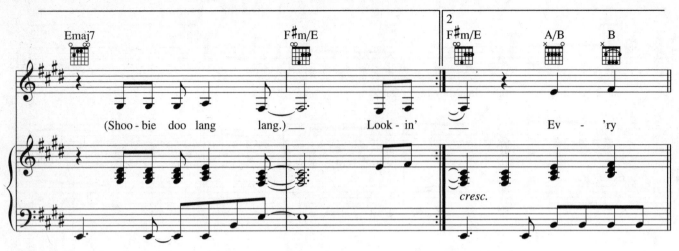

(Shoo - bie doo lang   lang.) __ Look - in' __ Ev - 'ry

sha - la - la - la, __ ev - 'ry whoa __ whoa __ still shines. __

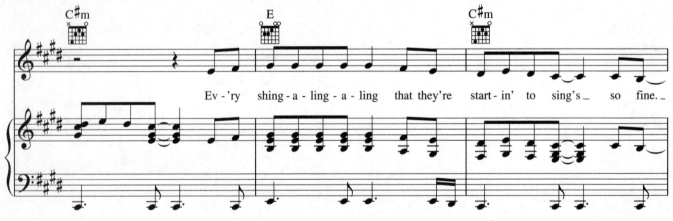

Ev - 'ry shing - a - ling - a - ling that they're start - in' to sing's __ so fine. __

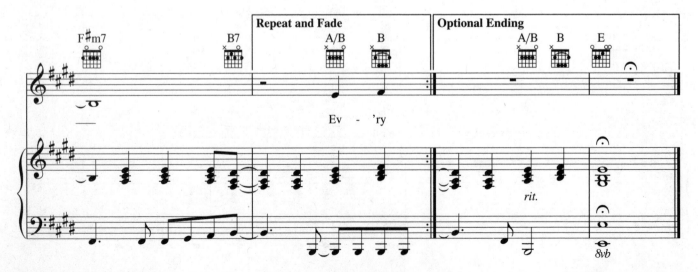

Ev - 'ry

YOU'D BE SO NICE TO COME HOME TO

from SOMETHING TO SHOUT ABOUT

Words and Music by
COLE PORTER

Moderately slow, with feeling

It's not that you're fair - er, than a lot of girls just as pleas - in', that I doff my hat as a wor - ship - per at your shrine. ___ It's

Classic Collections Of Your Favorite Songs

arranged for piano, voice, and guitar.

Beautiful Ballads

A massive collection of 87 songs, including: April in Paris • Autumn in New York • Call Me Irresponsible • Cry Me a River • I Wish You Love • I'll Be Seeing You • If • Imagine • Isn't It Romantic? • It's Impossible (Somos Novios) • Mona Lisa • Moon River • People • The Way We Were • A Whole New World (Aladdin's Theme) • and more.
00311679 ....$17.95

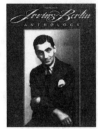

Irving Berlin Anthology

A comprehensive collection of 61 timeless songs with a bio, song background notes, and photos. Songs include: Always • Blue Skies • Cheek to Cheek • God Bless America • Marie • Puttin' on the Ritz • Steppin' Out with My Baby • There's No Business Like Show Business • White Christmas • (I Wonder Why?) You're Just in Love • and more.
00312493 ....$22.99

The Big Book of Standards

86 classics essential to any music library, including: April in Paris • Autumn in New York • Blue Skies • Cheek to Cheek • Heart and Soul • I Left My Heart in San Francisco • In the Mood • Isn't It Romantic? • Mona Lisa • Moon River • The Nearness of You • Out of Nowhere • Spanish Eyes • Star Dust • Stella by Starlight • That Old Black Magic • They Say It's Wonderful • What Now My Love • and more.
00311667 ....$19.95

Broadway Deluxe

This exciting collection of 125 of Broadway's biggest show tunes is deluxe indeed! Includes such showstoppers as: Bewitched • Cabaret • Camelot • Day by Day • Hello Young Lovers • I Could Have Danced All Night • I've Grown Accustomed to Her Face • If Ever I Would Leave You • The Lady Is a Tramp • I Talk to the Trees • My Heart Belongs to Daddy • Oklahoma • September Song • Seventy Six Trombones • Try to Remember • and more!
00309245 ....$24.95

The Great American Songbook – The Singers

Crooners, wailers, shouters, balladeers: some of our greatest pop vocalists have poured their hearts and souls into the musical gems of the Great American Songbook. This folio features 100 of these classics by Louis Armstrong, Tony Bennett, Rosemary Clooney, Nat "King" Cole, Bing Crosby, Doris Day, Ella Fitzgerald, Judy Garland, Dean Martin, Frank Sinatra, Barbra Streisand, Mel Tormé, and others.
00311433 ....$24.95

I'll Be Seeing You: 50 Songs of World War II

A salute to the music and memories of WWII, including a year-by-year chronology of events on the homefront, dozens of photos, and 50 radio favorites of the GIs and their families back home, including: Boogie Woogie Bugle Boy • Don't Sit Under the Apple Tree (With Anyone Else But Me) • I Don't Want to Walk Without You • I'll Be Seeing You • Moonlight in Vermont • There's a Star-Spangled Banner Waving Somewhere • You'd Be So Nice to Come Home To • and more.
00311698 ....$19.95

Lounge Music – 2nd Edition

Features over 50 top requests of the martini crowd: All the Way • Fever • I Write the Songs • Misty • Moon River • That's Amore (That's Love) • Yesterday • more.

00310193 ....$15.95

Best of Cole Porter

38 of his classics, including: All of You • Anything Goes • Be a Clown • Don't Fence Me In • I Get a Kick Out of You • In the Still of the Night • Let's Do It (Let's Fall in Love) • Night and Day • You Do Something to Me • and many more.
00311577 ....$14.95

Big Band Favorites

A great collection of 70 of the best Swing Era songs, including: East of the Sun • Honeysuckle Rose • I Can't Get Started with You • I'll Be Seeing You • In the Mood • Let's Get Away from It All • Moonglow • Moonlight in Vermont • Opus One • Stompin' at the Savoy • Tuxedo Junction • more!
00310445 ....$16.95

The Best of Rodgers & Hammerstein

A capsule of 26 classics from this legendary duo. Songs include: Climb Ev'ry Mountain • Edelweiss • Getting to Know You • I'm Gonna Wash That Man Right Outta My Hair • My Favorite Things • Oklahoma • The Surrey with the Fringe on Top • You'll Never Walk Alone • and more.
00308210 ....$16.95

The Best Songs Ever – 5th Edition

Over 70 must-own classics, including: All I Ask of You • Body and Soul • Crazy • Fly Me to the Moon • Here's That Rainy Day • Imagine • Love Me Tender • Memory • Moonlight in Vermont • My Funny Valentine • People • Satin Doll • Save the Best for Last • Tears in Heaven • A Time for Us • The Way We Were • What a Wonderful World • When I Fall in Love • and more.
00359224 .... $22.95

Torch Songs

Sing your heart out with this collection of 59 sultry jazz and big band melancholy masterpieces, including: Angel Eyes • Cry Me a River • I Can't Get Started • I Got It Bad and That Ain't Good • I'm Glad There Is You • Lover Man (Oh, Where Can You Be?) • Misty • My Funny Valentine • Stormy Weather • and many more! 224 pages.
00490446 ....$17.95

www.halleonard.com

Get more BANG for your buck!
with budgetbooks

These value-priced collections feature **over 300 pages** of **piano/vocal/guitar** arrangements. With at least **70 hit songs** in most books, you pay **18 cents or less** for each song!

Prices, contents & availability subject to change without notice.

FOR MORE INFORMATION,
SEE YOUR LOCAL MUSIC DEALER,
OR WRITE TO:

HAL•LEONARD®
CORPORATION
7777 W. BLUEMOUND RD. P.O. BOX 13819
MILWAUKEE, WISCONSIN 53213

www.halleonard.com

ACOUSTIC
66 unplugged jewels: American Pie • Blackbird • Leaving on a Jet Plane • More Than Words • Scarborough Fair • Tears in Heaven • Time in a Bottle • Wonderwall • more.
00311857 P/V/G $12.99

BLUES SONGS
99 blues classics packed into one affordable collection! Includes: All Your Love • Born Under a Bad Sign • Killing Floor • Pride and Joy • Sweet Home Chicago • The Thrill Is Gone • more!
00311499 P/V/G $12.95

BROADWAY SONGS
This jam-packed collection features 73 songs from 56 shows, including: Any Dream Will Do • Cabaret • Getting to Know You • I Dreamed a Dream • One • People • You'll Never Walk Alone • and more.
00310832 P/V/G $12.95

CHILDREN'S SONGS
This fabulous collection includes over 100 songs that kids love, including: Alphabet Song • London Bridge • On Top of Spaghetti • Sesame Street Theme • You've Got a Friend in Me • and more.
00311054 P/V/G $12.95

CHRISTMAS SONGS
100 holiday favorites, includes: All I Want for Christmas Is You • Away in a Manger • Feliz Navidad • The First Noel • Merry Christmas, Darling • O Holy Night • Silver Bells • What Child Is This? • and more.
00310887 P/V/G $12.95

CLASSIC ROCK
A priceless collection of 70 of rock's best at a price that can't be beat! Includes: Ballroom Blitz • Bohemian Rhapsody • Gloria • Pink Houses • Rhiannon • Roxanne • Summer of '69 • Wild Thing • You Really Got Me • and more.
00310906 P/V/G $12.95

CONTEMPORARY CHRISTIAN
52 CCM faves in a value-priced songbook: All to You • Be Near • Breathe • Deeper • I Wanna Sing • King • Maker of All Things • Oceans from the Rain • Pray • Song of Love • These Hands • Wisdom • more.
00311732 P/V/G $12.95

CONTEMPORARY HITS
A cost-saving collection of 53 favorites, including: Amazed • Angel • Breathe • Clocks • Don't Know Why • Drops of Jupiter (Tell Me) • A Moment Like This • Smooth • Superman (It's Not Easy) • Underneath It All • and more.
00311053 P/V/G $12.95

COUNTRY SONGS
A great collection of 90 songs, including: Always on My Mind • Amazed • Boot Scootin' Boogie • Down at the Twist and Shout • Friends in Low Places • Okie from Muskogee • Sixteen Tons • Walkin' After Midnight • You Are My Sunshine • and more.
00310833 P/V/G $12.99

EARLY ROCK
You can't go wrong with this collection of over 90 early rock classics, including: All Shook Up • Blue Suede Shoes • Bye Bye Love • Fun, Fun, Fun • Hello Mary Lou • Hound Dog • In My Room • Louie, Louie • Peggy Sue • Shout • Splish Splash • Tequila • and more.
00311055 P/V/G $12.95

FOLK SONGS
148 of your all-time folk favorites! Includes: Camptown Races • Danny Boy • Greensleeves • Home on the Range • Shenandoah • Skip to My Lou • Yankee Doodle • and many more.
00311841 P/V/G $12.99

GOSPEL SONGS
Over 100 songs, including: Behold the Lamb • Down by the Riverside • Daddy Sang Bass • In Times like These • Midnight Cry • We Are So Blessed • The Wonder of It All • and many more.
00311734 P/V/G $12.95

HYMNS
150 beloved hymns in a money-saving collection: Amazing Grace • Come, Thou Fount of Every Blessing • For the Beauty of the Earth • Holy, Holy, Holy • O Worship the King • What a Friend We Have in Jesus • many more!
00311587 P/V/G $12.99

JAZZ STANDARDS
A collection of over 80 jazz classics. Includes: Alfie • Bewitched • Blue Skies • Body and Soul • Fever • I'll Be Seeing You • In the Mood • Isn't It Romantic? • Mona Lisa • Stella by Starlight • When Sunny Gets Blue • and more.
00310830 P/V/G $12.95

LATIN SONGS
An invaluable collection of over 80 Latin standards. Includes: Desafinado (Off Key) • Frenesí • How Insensitive (Insensatez) • La Bamba • Perfidia • Spanish Eyes • So Nice (Summer Samba) • and more.
00311056 P/V/G $12.95

LOVE SONGS
This collection of over 70 favorite love songs includes: And I Love Her • Crazy • Endless Love • Longer • (You Make Me Feel Like) A Natural Woman • You Are So Beautiful • You Are the Sunshine of My Life • and more.
00310834 P/V/G $12.95

MOVIE SONGS
Over 70 memorable movie moments, including: Almost Paradise • Cole's Song • Funny Girl • Puttin' On the Ritz • She • Southampton • Take My Breath Away (Love Theme) • Up Where We Belong • The Way We Were • and more.
00310831 P/V/G $12.99

POP/ROCK
This great collection of 75 top pop hits features: Barbara Ann • Crimson and Clover • Dust in the Wind • Hero • Jack and Diane • Lady Marmalade • Stand by Me • Tequila • We Got the Beat • What's Going On • and more.
00310835 P/V/G $12.99

SHOWTUNES
80 songs, including: And All That Jazz • Camelot • Easter Parade • Hey, Look Me Over • I Remember It Well • If I Were a Rich Man • Try to Remember • Why Can't You Behave? • Wouldn't It Be Loverly • and more.
00311849 P/V/G $12.99

STANDARDS
Nearly 80 standards, including: Boogie Woogie Bugle Boy • Don't Get Around Much Anymore • In the Still of the Night • Misty • Pennies from Heaven • So in Love • What a Diff'rence a Day Made • Witchcraft • and more.
00311853 P/V/G $12.99

1009